S0-CCE-862

Daryl Kahn Cline
July 30, 1983
Harvard Coop
Boston

LET'S
TALK
ABOUT
IT

LET'S TALK ABOUT IT

MYRNA KNEPLER

Northeastern Illinois University

HARCOURT BRACE JOVANOVICH, INC.

New York   San Diego   Chicago   San Francisco   Atlanta
London   Sydney   Toronto

To Henry, who supported and helped.

*To daughters, friends, and colleagues whose names
appear scattered throughout the text.*

Illustrations by Susan Stillman

Copyright © 1982 by Harcourt Brace Jovanovich, Inc.

All rights reserved. No part of this publication may be reproduced or transmitted in any form or
by any means, electronic or mechanical, including photocopy, recording, or any information
storage and retrieval system, without permission in writing from the publisher.

Requests for permission to make copies of any part of the work should be mailed to:
Permissions, Harcourt Brace Jovanovich, Inc., 757 Third Avenue, New York, N.Y. 10017.

ISBN: 0-15-550585-8

Library of Congress Catalog Card Number: 81-83105

Printed in the United States of America

TO THE STUDENT

The purpose of this book is to help you to talk about your ideas and opinions in English.

All of you know quite a lot of English by now. You probably can carry on short conversations with English speakers, but perhaps it is still difficult for you to talk about the more complicated thoughts and ideas that come easily to your mind in your own language.

This book will give you practice in carrying on adult conversations and discussions in English. In addition, it will help you to review some of the grammar points that often cause difficulties for students of the language.

Many of the exercises ask you to express your own ideas and opinions. Because different people have different ideas, there will always be more than one answer to each question. Each answer you give, however, must be in a correct grammatical form. If you need help with the grammar, the teacher will refer you to one of the special grammar exercises in Section Three.

TO THE TEACHER

This book is designed to help students learn to carry on extended conversations in English—the kinds of conversations that take place among adults in the college classroom, or among co-workers discussing a job to be done, or among friends, once pleasantries have been exchanged.

The book is written with the intermediate student of English in mind. That is to say, it is for the student who has already been taught most of the common grammatical patterns of English and can produce many of them with some degree of accuracy. This student also commands a sufficient vocabulary to perform the tasks of everyday life and carry on short social conversations in English.

But "survival English" is not enough for many students. If the students are adults and used to discussing adult ideas in their own language, they may be frustrated by their inability to do so in English. They may either feel forced to talk what they consider "baby talk" in English or to remain silent just when they feel the need to speak.

Most students find it easier to speak if there is some framework for conversation. In this book that framework is provided by the short text that begins each lesson. This text, in the form of a story, presents either a series of events in someone's life for comment and speculation (Section One) or a problem to be solved (Section Two). It is hoped that some of the texts are lively enough to make students smile occasionally. Each chapter in Section One focuses on one or more grammatical structures that frequently cause difficulties for intermediate-level students. In both sections the conversation exercises first center on the students' reactions to the events or problems in the stories and then lead to opportunities for students to talk about their own ideas and experiences.

All the exercises in Sections One and Two are aimed at getting students to actively create their own utterances, using their own understanding and imagination. There is never any one correct answer; there are always many. The exercises in Section One lead students toward framing their answers in the form of particular structural patterns; in Section Two there are no such constraints.

The final section consists of sixteen mini-grammars, one for each lesson in Section One. Each mini-grammar contains a short explanation of the corresponding lesson, as well as exercises to reinforce learning.

The book can be used in several ways. It can be the main text in a conversation class, perhaps supplemented by listening comprehension and pronunciation exercises. Alternatively, it can be used as a grammar review in a course emphasizing communicative competence.

Most of the exercises can be used in a number of different ways. Students may work individually, reporting their answers to the class; they may work with a partner, or in small groups. The emphasis is on oral work, but many of the exercises can also be written out for further practice. Some exercises can even be developed into composition topics if such activity is consistent with the goals of the class. More detailed suggestions to the teacher follow.

Suggestions for using Section One

Section One emphasizes the use of appropriate grammatical structures in a conversational context. Each lesson contains:

1. A listing of structure skills needed to do the conversation exercises in that lesson.

2. A short text in the form of a story.

3. Conversation exercises based on the situation or problem in the story. Each exercise demands mastery of a particular grammatical structure, but leaves students free to develop their own answers as long as they are appropriate to the situation.

4. Conversation exercises based on the students' own experiences.

5. Vocabulary expansion exercises (in most lessons).

There are several ways in which the lessons in Section One may be used, depending on the teacher's style and the ability level of the students. Since most of the conversation exercises are based on the story that begins each lesson, students should understand it completely. It is probably best to read the story aloud at least once, with the students following it in their books. Definitions of difficult words can be elicited from the class and written on the blackboard. Some factual questions about the text should be asked, and one or more students can be asked to summarize it.

In low-intermediate classes, the teacher may wish to do some of the appropriate grammer review exercises from the corresponding mini-grammar (in Section Three) with the class before beginning the conversation exercises. Some teachers may also wish to assign grammar exercises to be done at home before the class meetings.

In working with more advanced students, the teacher may move directly into the conversation exercises. The mini-grammers can then be used independently by students when they need help with a particular structure, and by the teacher if the majority of the class shows weakness on a particular grammar point.

Most of the conversation exercises can be done either by having individual students report their answers to the class or by assigning partners and giving each pair a few minutes to develop answers together. A few of the exercises call for role plays, which can be rehearsed with a partner and then performed in front of the class.

Even though the focus of the book is on oral communication, the teacher may want to assign some conversation exercises as written classwork or homework from time to time in order to check student progress.

Suggestion for using Section Two

The lessons in Section Two are constructed somewhat differently from those in Section One. In Section Two students are not asked to respond to a particular grammatical form, although they will probably call upon forms learned in earlier lessons.

Each text in Section Two describes a problem, the solution of which is the basis for class discussion. The problem is in narrative form because students seem to be able to respond more easily to such stories than to abstract discussion topics; instead of asking students to talk about the advantages and disadvantages of moving to a new place, a lesson asks the student to decide whether a particular family, as described in the story, should pull up stakes.

Except for very small classes, most of the lessons in Section Two are probably taught most successfully if the students are divided into small groups to work out the answers to the problems together. Many students find it easier to speak in such small groups, and such conversations are closer to experience outside the classroom. Three to five students per group seems to work best. Each group should have a chairperson in charge of reporting the group's decision to the class. In the first class sessions the teacher should be responsible for setting up the groups and selecting chairpersons from among the most verbally skillful students. Later the responsibility of arranging groups and selecting chairpersons can be shared with the class, although every member should have a chance to lead a group.

Teachers will find many ways of working with these materials. A detailed plan for teaching the first lesson in Section Two, "Moving to Another City," is provided only as a guide.

Teaching "Moving to Another City"

FIRST DAY

1. *Warm-up:* "Many of you have moved here recently. It's difficult to move, isn't it? Were there some problems?"

2. Write *difficult vocabulary* on the board. Definitions can be elicited either before or after the first reading of the text.

3. *Read story aloud* at least once, while students look at their copies. Ask factual questions about details of the story. Ask one or more of the students to summarize the main points. Do not attempt to use the story as a listening comprehension exercise only; students need to have the text in front of them to be aware of all the details they must consider.

4. *Set the problem:* "What do the Thompsons have to decide? Do different members of the family want different things?"

5. *Ask students to read over the problem at home.*

SECOND DAY

6. *Divide the class* into groups of three to five students. Select a chairperson for each group to report to the class.

7. *Explain* that each group has two tasks: (1) to decide the best solution to the problem, (2) to give several good reasons for their decision. There is no right answer. If members of a group disagree (and you hope they will), each person should try to convince the rest of the group. Emphasize that while the chairperson of each group will make the report, everyone in the group must contribute to the solution.

8. Groups begin their discussion. Tell them they must be ready to report their decision and reasons in 10 minutes. Setting a time limit for the discussion is important. During the group discussion:
   (a) Circulate rapidly to see that each group understands its task and is beginning.
   (b) Visit each group to see that the members of the group are working toward a common solution. If agreement comes too quickly, be prepared to play devil's advocate.
   (c) Visit each group one more time to check to see that the group can give reasons for its decision.

9. The chairperson of each group *reports to the class.* Then the floor is open for class discussion and comments. It is sometimes good to run a little short of time. (I like to have my students still arguing as they leave the classroom).

THIRD DAY

10. Do "Questions for Discussion" as follow-up.

Suggestions for using Section Three

The sixteen mini-grammars of Section Three are keyed to the sixteen lessons in Section One. Each contains a short explanation of the grammar needed to complete the lesson, and exercises to reinforce the learning of that grammar. Unlike the exercises in Section One, which focus on communication, the exercises in the mini-grammars focus on the learning of the appropriate grammatical structure. They can generally be expected to be easier than the exercises in Section One.

In more advanced classes the teacher will probably want to begin with the lessons of Section One and use the mini-grammars only when needed. Teachers working with low-intermediate level students, however, may wish to teach all or part of a mini-grammar before beginning the corresponding lesson in Section One.

ACKNOWLEDGMENTS

I would like to thank Len Fox of Brooklyn College and Carol G. Rossi of the University of Santa Clara for their helpful comments.

Two people at Harcourt Brace Jovanovich deserve special thanks: Albert Richards, for his enthusiasm and his helpful ideas about the project, and Andrea Haight, whose careful queries, intelligent suggestions, and constant support were of great value to me. I am no less grateful to Jeremiah Lighter and Nancy E. Kalal for their essential contributions: creating the book's design and overseeing its production.

MYRNA KNEPLER

CONTENTS

Section Two   Problem-Solving Exercises   69

Section Three   Mini-grammars   89

ONE

SITUATIONS
FOR
DISCUSSION

1

STRUCTURE SKILLS
Forming negative sentences

Opposites Attract

Steve and Jeff are good friends although they are completely different from each other. Steve is very short and rather fat. He likes to wear bright-colored casual clothes. Last week he bought a flashy red plaid shirt and a loud print tie. He also bought an expensive pair of shiny leather shoes. Every week Steve spends his paycheck before he gets another one.

Steve enjoys being with people. He's extremely cheerful all the time and likes to tell jokes. People laugh at his jokes, but he laughs even harder. His laugh is very loud.

Steve loves to go to parties. He eats and drinks a lot and is always surrounded by people. He likes to dance and to listen to loud music. At every party he sings all his favorite songs at the top of his voice and dances with all the girls in the room. He's the last one to leave any party. Steve is a typical extrovert.

EXERCISES

1. Jeff is Steve's best friend. He is completely different from Steve in looks, personality, and habits. Describe Jeff, keeping all your sentences affirmative but using words with meanings that are opposite in meaning to some of the words in the story (antonyms). You may use your imagination to add additional details to your story.

> **EXAMPLE:** Jeff is very tall and rather thin. . . .
>
> He is a typical introvert.

2. Describe Jeff again, this time using negative sentences whenever possible.

> **EXAMPLE:** Jeff is not short and not fat.
>
> He doesn't like to wear bright-colored clothes.

3. How many untrue statements can you make? One student deliberately makes an untrue statement. The next student must immediately change it to a true statement by changing affirmative to negative or negative to affirmative.

EXAMPLES: The earth is flat. (first student)

The earth isn't flat. (second student)

This room doesn't have a door. (first student)

This room has a door. (second student)

4. After many years of working in a snack shop, Mr. Miller and his wife were able to open a small restaurant of their own a few years ago. Although their business has been fairly successful, both of them have had to work ten to twelve hour days, six days a week. Mr. Miller buys all the food and even does some of the cooking. He is always concerned that his customers are satisfied and likes to visit their tables and chat with them. After everyone else has gone home Mr. Miller plans the next day's menus. Many evenings the Millers don't leave the restaurant until after midnight.

Last summer, the Millers took their first vacation in years. During those three weeks they lived in a completely different way than usual. Tell at least ten things the Millers didn't do on their vacation.

EXAMPLE: They didn't get up at 6:00. Instead, they slept until ten.

5. All last semester, My Hanh worked part-time as a cashier in the neighborhood drugstore and took a full load of courses at the junior college downtown. She was always rushing from place to place. This summer she will still be working but she won't be going to school for three months. It will seem like a vacation to her. What are some things My Hanh won't do this summer?

EXAMPLE: She won't buy her lunch from a vending machine. She will have time to prepare herself a good meal.

6. Do you think it is really possible for people who are as different from one another as Steve and Jeff to be good friends? Do you have any friends whose personality and habits are very different from your own? How are they different from yours?

7. Do you think husbands and wives should have similar personalities and interests? Do you know of a successful marriage in which the husband and wife are very different?

Vocabulary: Antonyms
Antonyms are words with opposite or nearly opposite meanings such as:

loud   soft   casual   formal   extrovert   introvert

The antonyms for many English words can be formed by adding prefixes such as: *un-, in-, im-*.

pleasant	unpleasant
patient	impatient
credible	incredible

Supply the antonyms for the following words. Then use each word in a sentence. If you are not certain which prefix to use, check your dictionary.

worthy	conspicuous	credible
comfortable	sensitive	equal
lucky	predictable	fit
possible	known	separable

LESSON

STRUCTURE SKILLS
Forming questions

Tommy

Tommy is four years old. That's the age when children usually ask a lot of questions. Every time Tommy goes somewhere with his parents, he pulls on their hands and asks a million questions, "What is that? Where are those people going? When are we going to leave? Why is the sky blue?" Tommy asks questions about everyone and everything. His mother and father get very tired.

Tommy even asks questions that adults consider rude. Last week he asked a middle-aged woman, "How old are you?" She didn't answer. When his father's boss came to dinner, Tommy asked, "Why is he so fat? What smells?" (The guest was smoking a cigar.) One day he asked his aunt, whom he loved very much, "Why are you wearing such a funny dress?"

Maybe when Tommy grows up he won't ask so many questions, but maybe he will. People learn things by asking questions.

EXERCISES

1. Think of ten more questions that Tommy might ask.

2. Imagine you are a visitor from another planet. You have just walked into the classroom and you have never seen a room like it or people like your fellow students. All rooms on Planet X are spherical and every person has a single eye in the middle of his forehead. You are very curious about the strange people you see on earth. Think of ten questions to ask them.

3. Choose a famous person that you would like to interview. It may be a movie star, a famous author, the head of a government, or any other prominent figure. You are a reporter who has just been given permission to do the interview. What questions do you want to ask?

4. Divide into groups of two. The person on the left is the reporter. The reporter has five minutes to find out as much about his classmate as possible by asking questions. Students being interviewed should answer only those questions they want to answer.* Later the reporter and the interviewee can change places.

5. *Role play: Travel bureau.* One student plays a travel agent; the other student plays the customer. The customer asks about a place to go for a vacation, and the travel agent suggests his own home town or another place with which he is very familiar. The customer asks as many questions as he can think of about transportation, hotel accommodations, weather, foods to try, points of interest, and so on. (The first time the exercise is done, the teacher may assume one of the roles.)

6. Listen to a radio or television news broadcast with your classmates. (The broadcast can be recorded by the teacher and played in class, or students can be asked to make their own arrangements for listening to a particular news program.) Prepare a variety of questions:

    a. some questions that can be answered *yes* or *no*

    b. some questions asking for information and beginning wih the words *where, when, why,* and *how*

    c. some questions beginning wih the words *who* and *what* referring to the object

    d. some questions beginning wih the words *who* and *what* referring to the subject

(In class, individual students can be asked to write their questions on the board for discussion, or students can work in groups to write a series of questions about a particular news item.)

7. In different countries people have different ideas about what questions a polite person may ask a stranger. In the country in which you grew up is it considered polite to ask a person you have just met, about: his age, his health, his job, the amount of money he makes, whether or not he is married? Are there some personal questions you might ask someone your own age or younger that you would not ask an older person? Are there some questions you would not ask a person of higher status than your own but might ask someone you felt to be your equal?

---

* It is very important that everyone understand that students have a right to refuse to answer any questions they might find embarrassing. There are some questions that most people would consider too personal and would not want to answer.

Vocabulary

Following are some words used to describe a person's age. Tell the approximate age range (in years) of a person described as:

an infant	an elderly man or woman
a child	an aged man or woman
an adolescent	a middle-aged man or woman
a teenager	a young man or woman
a youth	a man in his thirties
an adult	a woman in her late twenties

3

STRUCTURE SKILLS
Ways of talking about future time

A Long Sleep

Ralph is now thirty years old. Tomorrow he is going to drink a magic liquid that will allow him to sleep for twenty years and wake up when he is fifty years old.

Of course when he wakes up twenty years from now, the world will have changed a great deal. He will look different, and so will his wife. His children, who are now very young, will have become adults and will have moved away from home. The new car that he bought a few months ago will be old and rusted. His new house will need repairs. His clothes will look very old-fashioned. The city he lives in will look very different. There will be many new tall buildings and many of the landmarks he knows will have disappeared.

Ralph will probably be very confused by all the new things he is going to see. It will take him a while to get used to living in the twenty-first century.

EXERCISES

1. Name ten more changes that Ralph will notice when he wakes up twenty years from now.

2. What are your plans for this coming weekend? Where are you going to go? What are you going to do?

3. What are you planning to do during the next school vacation? Are you going to travel or stay where you are? What new things will you have time to do?

4. Name five things that you would like to learn to do in the next few years. How are you going to learn them?

5. How do you think your life will be different five years from now? Will you still be going to school? Will you know English almost perfectly? Will you be living in the same place? Either give a short talk or write a short composition called "A Day in My Life in 19——." Of course no one knows for certain what is going to happen in the future, but tell what you think a typical day will be like.

6. Think about a small child that you know. It can be someone in your own family or the child of a friend. How will his or her life be different when he or she is your age? Will some things be easier? Will other things be more difficult?

7. In the last hundred years many new things have been invented: the automobile, radio and television, the airplane, the skyscraper, and the cures for diseases. Can you think of some things that might be invented or improved in the next hundred years?

8. Have you ever read a science fiction story or seen a movie or television show about the world of the future? Tell about some of the events in a science fiction story you know.

Vocabulary: Idiomatic verbal expressions

Sometimes a group of words taken as a whole will have a special meaning that is different from the meaning of the individual words. For example, in the sentence "The grocery store has *run out of* milk," the meanings of the separate words *run, out,* and *of* are not related to the meaning of the expression *run out of.* What the sentence means is that the store usually has milk for sale but does not have any now.

Here are some other expressions with special meanings:

    to talk back to (to answer impolitely)

    to get along with someone (to be friendly with, act harmoniously with)

    to keep one's head (to remain calm)

    to keep an eye on someone or something (to watch)

    to drop in on someone (to visit someone without notice)

    to put one's foot in one's mouth (to say something foolish without thinking)

    to not mind (to not be disturbed by)

Construct a new sentence with approximately the same meaning as the sentence given. Use the appropriate form of one of the idiomatic verbal expressions above in your sentence.

EXAMPLE: Steve is friendly with Jeff.

Steve gets along with Jeff.

a. Tommy decided to visit his friend without notice.

b. A person who talks without thinking often says foolish things.

c. Teen-agers sometimes answer their parents impolitely.

d. It is important to remain calm in emergencies.

e. Some people are not disturbed by Tommy's questions.

f. Tommy's mother asked a neighbor to watch Tommy for a few minutes.

STRUCTURE SKILLS

Used to + the simple form of the verb to express
a habitual state or action in the past

The Good Old Days

Grandpa Smith likes to reminisce about the days when he was a young man. "When I was your age," he tells his teen-age grandchildren, "life ~~wasn't so easy~~. I never had a car. I used to walk three miles to school every day. After school I had to work around my father's farm. I used to feed all the animals and clean the stalls. Every evening I used to chop wood for the fire. On weekends I used to help wih the milking."

Grandpa Smith also objects to his grandchildren's behavior. "When I was your age," he tells them, "I never used to talk back to my parents. I respected older people. I used to do everything they said."

Grandpa Smith really loves his grandchildren, but that doesn't mean that he always agrees with them.

EXERCISES

1. What other things do you think Grandpa Smith used to do when he was a young man?

2. Grandpa Smith's oldest grandson, Fred, is now eighteen. The day after his birthday the family looked at old pictures and talked about the things Fred used to do when he was younger. Name some things you think Fred used to do when he was six months old. Two years old. Eight years old. Twelve years old.

3. Ben has worked at the same factory since he was a young man. Forty years ago he organized a strike that led to the formation of a union. For several years his co-workers have elected him their union representative.

When Ben first started work, conditions in the factory were very bad. Workers could be laid off without notice; no one was paid for extra work; ventilation was bad; the machines were extremely noisy and some of them were even dangerous. Nowadays, working conditions are much better and much safer.

Imagine you are Ben describing conditions in the factory as they used to be, and as they are now.

4. Talk about some things that you used to do in the past but no longer do.

> **EXAMPLES:** I used to smoke a pack of cigarettes a day.
>
> I used to believe my parents were perfect. I still love them, but I know they are only human.

5. Have your parents or older relatives ever talked to you about their lives when they were younger? What did they use to do in their youth that they no longer do?

Vocabulary: Two-word verbs
Here are some common two-word verbs and their meanings:

call on (ask to recite)

get off (descend from)

get on (enter [a bus or train])

get over (recover from)

get up (rise)

keep on (continue)

look into (investigate)

run into (meet by chance)

run across (find by chance)

Construct new sentences with approximately the same meanings as the sentences given, using the appropriate form of a two-word verb.

> **EXAMPLE:** Sarah *entered* the bus when it stopped at her corner.
>
> Sarah *got on* the bus when it stopped at her corner.

a. Anne *met* her friend *by chance* near the restaurant.

b. Mrs. Thompson *rises* early every weekday morning.

c. The teacher *asked* Ben *to recite.*

d. Susan has *recovered from* her cold.

e. Roger *continued* studying after his roommates had fallen asleep.

f. If you *happen to find* that book about Mexico, please tell me.

g. All passengers must *descend from* the train at the terminal.

h. The police *investigated* the robbery.

STRUCTURE SKILLS
Be used to + verb + -ing

Adverbs of frequency

A Man of Habit

Mr. M. is a man of habit. He always does the same things day in and day out. His alarm clock rings at 7:15 every morning, and at 7:18 sharp he jumps out of bed and takes a shower. He does exactly five minutes of exercise every morning while he watches his favorite news broadcast. Then he puts on a conservative three piece suit, a striped tie, and dark shoes, and goes down for breakfast.

Every morning he has two cups of coffee with three lumps of sugar in each, toast with butter, and a small glass of orange juice. His wife has been making him exactly the same breakfast for twenty years. After breakfast, Mr. M. usually smokes one cigarette. He has been smoking the same brand since he was a young man.

At 8:32 every morning, Mr. M. kisses his wife twice on the right cheek and leaves for his job at the bank. He is never late.

Yesterday, Mrs. M. said she was bored with their routine life. Mr. M. became very angry. "Why should I change?" he said. "I'm used to doing things a certain way, and I like it."

EXERCISES

1. Mr. M. likes his routine. He is used to doing the same things day after day. Name ten or more activities mentioned in the story that Mr. M. is used to doing.

EXAMPLE: He is used to hearing his alarm clock ring at 7:15.

2. The story only tells about Mr. M.'s activities in the morning. In fact, Mr. M. follows his routine all day long. Imagine what Mr. M. is used to doing after he leaves his house every morning. Construct five or more sentences about Mr. M.'s routine after he leaves his house.

EXAMPLE: He is used to parking his car in the bank's parking lot.

3. Mrs. M. does not have as regular a schedule as her husband. She is a housewife, but she also teaches a class at a local college. This is Mrs. M.'s schedule:

Every day: gets up at 7:00 a.m., makes breakfast, does the breakfast dishes, listens to the weather forecast on the radio, makes the beds, reads the newspaper, cleans the house a little

Most days: takes the bus to work, teaches a class, grades students' papers, eats lunch in the college cafeteria, watches the news on TV

Several times a month: shops at the supermarket, cleans the house thoroughly, has lunch in an inexpensive restaurant with a friend, gives her students a test, plays tennis, goes to a faculty meeting, goes to the movies

A few times a year: has her hair cut in the beauty shop, visits her sister in another town, eats dinner in an expensive restaurant, invites a dozen friends to her house for a party, goes to the theater.

There are also some things that Mrs. M. doesn't ever do:

She doesn't ever eat breakfast in a restaurant.

She doesn't ever read a newspaper in class.

She doesn't play football.

She doesn't act on TV.

She doesn't invite a dozen friends to dinner at an expensive restaurant.

Construct several sentences telling what Mrs. M. is used to doing. (Your sentences do not have to be about things Mrs. M. does every day. They can be about things she does less often, but regularly.)

EXAMPLES: Mrs. M. is used to eating lunch in the school cafeteria on weekdays.

Mrs. M. is used to having her hair cut at the beauty shop a few times a year.

4. Name several things that Mrs. M. always does. Usually does. Sometimes does. Seldom does. Never does.

5. Think about your own routine. Write three sentences each about: the things that you always do, the things you often do, the things you sometimes do, the things you seldom do, and the things you never do. (You should have a total of fifteen sentences.)

6. Compare the sentences you wrote in Exercise 5 with those of another student. Together construct sentences that tell about both of your routines.

> EXAMPLES: I always take the bus to school, but Marie seldom does.
>
> Both Maria and I usually study in the library.
>
> Sometimes we study together.
>
> Neither of us plays golf.

7. Give a short talk (or write a short composition) called "My Routine." Do not try to talk about everything you do regularly. Select a few activities and give additional details about them.

8. Describe the routine of someone you know well: a friend or a relative.

Vocabulary: Additional adverbs of frequency

Here are a few more words that are used to talk about how often things happen.

almost always	occasionally
frequently	rarely
often	hardly ever

Construct sentences of your own using each of these words. You may want to talk about events at your school.

LESSON
6

STRUCTURE SKILLS
Special meanings of <u>make</u>, <u>let</u>, and <u>have</u> followed by
the simple form of the next verb

The Browns

Mr. and Mrs. Brown have two young children. Both parents work, and three days a week Mrs. Brown leaves her job a little early to take care of the children when they come home from school. On the other days Mr. Brown watches the children after school.

The Browns get along well, but they don't always agree on how to raise their children. Mrs. Brown is very strict. She makes the children follow a lot of rules. Mr. Brown is very permissive. He often lets the children do what they want.

Mrs. Brown makes the children do their homework the minute they get home from school. She doesn't let them watch television very much. She makes them keep their clothes clean and their rooms neat. She never lets them eat candy between meals.

Mr. Brown lets the children play before they do their homework. He lets them watch as much television as they want, and he doesn't make them turn the sound down. He lets them wear dirty clothes when they are playing and he doesn't mind if their rooms are a little bit messy. When they are good he takes them to the store and lets them buy candy.

Weekends are very busy times for the Browns. Both parents work at cleaning up the apartment. They take turns doing the grocery shopping. If there is time, the whole family goes someplace special in the afternoon. One weekend evening the parents like to go out by themselves. They have someone take care of the children while they are gone. They usually have the baby-sitter prepare a light meal, play with the children for a while, and put them to bed. After working hard all week, the Browns deserve a night out.

EXERCISES

1. Think of five things not mentioned in the story that Mrs. Brown probably makes her children do.

Also think of five things she probably doesn't let them do.

2. Think of five things not mentioned in the story that Mr. Brown probably lets the children do.

Also think of five things he probably doesn't make them do.

3. *Role Play*: One student takes the role of the permissive parent; another student is the strict parent. Three other students play their children who are six, ten, and sixteen years old. The children take turns making requests which the parents each answer according to their roles.

EXAMPLES: Sixteen year old: $\begin{Bmatrix} \text{May} \\ \text{Can} \end{Bmatrix}$* I go out this evening?

Permissive parent: Of course, you need to have some fun.

Strict parent: Of course not, tomorrow is a school day.

4. The Blantons are average parents. They are neither very strict nor very permissive. They have two boys, one seventeen and one twelve. Because of the difference in the children's ages, the Blantons let their older son do many things that they don't let their younger son do. For example, the seventeen year old son may watch television as late as he likes, but the twelve year old must turn off the television set before 10:00 p.m. What are some other things that you think average parents should let a seventeen-year-old do, but should not let a younger child do?

5. Judy works from nine to five. She's a secretary in a large office. Although she likes many of the people she works with, she doesn't like her boss. It seems that every few minutes he is interrupting her work to have her do little extra jobs for him. Most of these jobs are not very important, and she thinks that he could do them himself or have someone else do them for him. Judy often has to work overtime to get her own work done.

Judy is thinking of complaining about her boss's behavior and has begun to talk about the problem with her co-workers. List some of Judy's complaints.

EXAMPLE: He has me make his dentist appointments. That's not part of my job description.

Complete the list with as many items as possible.

6. When you go the barber (beauty) shop, what do you have the barber (beautician) do? (wash hair, cut hair, tint hair, curl hair, give permanent, give manicure, give shave)

---

* Both *can* and *may* are used by educated speakers of English to ask for permission. *May* is considered more formal.

7. When you stop at a gas station what do you have the attendant do? (fill the gas tank, check oil, change oil, check air pressure in the tires, clean windshield)

8. Do you think it is better for children to have strict parents or permissive parents? Do you think children are raised more or less strictly in the country where you grew up than they are in the United States?

LESSON

7

STRUCTURE SKILLS

Wishes about present or future events

Hopes about present or future events

Giving advice about present or future events using <u>should</u>, <u>ought to</u>, and <u>had better</u>

Susan

Susan is an American high school student. She is slightly overweight. She doesn't like the color of her hair, which is brown.

Every month she buys a lot of fashion magazines that show pictures of slim models wearing beautiful clothes. Susan is so busy reading these magazines and watching her favorite television shows that she often forgets to wash her hair or take care of her clothes. While she reads the magazines she eats chocolate.

When Susan is not watching television, she talks for hours on the telephone with her friends.

EXERCISES

1. The story tells the facts about Susan's life. Sometimes we want to talk about things that we know are impossible, improbable, or contrary to fact. One way of doing this is to use *wish* plus a special form of the verb.

EXAMPLES: Susan wishes she were as thin as a fashion model.

Susan wishes she didn't like chocolates.

What are some more things you think Susan wishes?

2. Now imagine you are all Susan's friends. You would like Susan to change in the future, and you think it is possible for her to do so. Use the word *hope* in your answers.

EXAMPLE: I hope Susan will lose some weight next month.

3. *Role Play*: One student plays Susan. Another student is Susan's mother or father. The parent gives Susan advice, using the word *should.* Susan gives reasons for not doing what her parent wants.

EXAMPLE: Parent: You should wash your hair more often.

Susan: Well, I wash my hair often enough.

I don't have time to wash my hair.

4. Many newspapers in the United States publish an advice column. Readers send in letters about their personal problems. The columnist publishes some of the letters, along wih advice on how to solve the problems. If an English-language newspaper with an advice column is available to the class, look at the letters and the advice given. Do you agree with the advice? What other advice would you give? Use *should, ought to, had better, wish,* and *hope* in your answers.

5. Choose a situation in your own life where you have enough knowledge to give someone advice. (For example, you may be able to give good advice on how to find a job based on your own experience in looking for one, or you may be able to advise someone about how to do a particular job that you have already learned to do. You may be an expert in the differences in customs between your own country and another country you have lived in and may be able to give good advice about those differences.) Imagine someone you know has asked you for advice. Give as much advice as possible using *should, shouldn't, ought to,* and *had better.*

6. You may have found out by now that some of your classmates are experts on subjects you need to know about. Ask them for advice.

7. All of us wish for things that we know are not true now. Discuss with the class some of your own wishes. (Remember that your wishes must be contrary to fact. Don't say, "I wish I had a job," if you really do have one.)

8. Give a short talk or write a short composition explaining your hopes for the future. Tell what you intend to do to make some of those hopes become realities.

Vocabulary: Synonym practice
Susan is *overweight.* There are many words whose meaning is similiar to *overweight*:

fat	stocky
chubby	plump
stout	obese

All of these words could be used to describe Susan, but each word gives a slightly different picture of what Susan looks like. Use your all-English dictionary to see if you can discover any differences in meaning between these words. Discuss these differences with your teacher and classmates.

Most fashion models are *slim*. Other words that are similiar but not exactly the same as *slim* are:

underweight	scrawny
thin	slender
skinny	lean

Discuss the differences between these words in class. Are some words more complimentary than others? If you were describing a person whose appearance you liked, which of these words would you use?

8

STRUCTURE SKILLS
Wishes about past events

Possibility in the past using <u>could</u> + <u>have</u> + past participle

George

George was a famous star of the silent movies. He was very tall and handsome and had many leading roles. When he went out, hundreds of young women would gather around him. His picture was on the cover of many magazines. He became very rich and bought a huge home in Hollywood.

Then someone invented the talking movies. George had a terrible voice. He sounded like a chicken. He never made another movie.

EXERCISES

1. George is very unhappy about what happened to him after the talking movies were invented. He wishes that things had been different. Tell the class what you think he wishes had happened.

EXAMPLE: He wishes no one had invented the talking movies.

2. In your own life there were probably times when you had two different things you could have done, but you decided to do only one. Tell the class some things you really did and some things you could have done (but didn't do). Explain why you made your choice.

EXAMPLE: I decided to study English although I could have studied French. I knew I was going to study in the United States.

Vocabulary: Synonym practice

A long time ago, George bought a *huge* home in Hollywood. *Huge* means very large. There are several other words that have similar meanings:

enormous   immense   gigantic   vast

George's home in Hollywood had a *gigantic* swimming pool. It was five hundred feet long. Behind the swimming pool was a *vast* lawn where George played golf every day. On the other side of the house George kept several *huge* cars and an *enormous* yacht in an *immense* garage.

Using the vocabulary of this exercise, give a short talk or write a short composition describing something that you have seen that is very large (a city, a mountain, a waterfall, etc.).

LESSON

STRUCTURE SKILLS
Future conditions using if

Tom

Tom's father is a doctor, and ever since Tom was a little boy his parents have wanted Tom to become a doctor too. Tom, however, would rather be an artist. All his life Tom has loved to draw and paint. People say that he is very talented.

Tom's parents say it would be foolish for Tom to become an artist. His father tells him that doctors help people and artists don't. His mother tells him that artists don't make enough money to support themselves.

Tom is now in medical school, but he is not very happy. He doesn't mind the hard work, but he finds studying medicine very boring. He doesn't like hospitals, and he gets sick every time he sees blood.

Tom is still thinking of becoming a professional artist, but he isn't sure that he can do it. He doesn't know how he will support himself if his parents don't help him. He wishes he didn't have to worry about money. He wishes he could please himself and make his parents happy too.

EXERCISES

1. Tom has not decided what to do in the future. Several actions are possible. Complete the following sentences:

a. If Tom becomes an artist, he will _____ .

b. If Tom quits medical school, his parents will _____ .

c. If Tom remains in medical school, he will _____ .

d. If Tom stops painting, he will _____ .

e. If Tom stops painting, his parents will _____ .

2. Tom knows that it is impossible to change some things in his life, but he still thinks about what would happen if conditions were different. Complete Tom's thoughts:

a. If my parents thought painting was important, they would _____ .

b. If medical school weren't so boring, I would _____ .

c. If artists made more money, I could _____ .

d. If I had my own money, I could _____ .

e. If I weren't so unhappy, I would _____ .

3. Jan is divorced and lives with her two young sons in a small city on the West coast. Her job as a telephone information operator is not very interesting and brings in just enough money to pay the bills.

A few days ago one of Jan's co-workers changed jobs. Jan's friend became the first woman in their branch of the company to work outdoors repairing telephone lines. Her salary is twenty-five percent higher than before, without any increase in hours. Jan's friend thinks that there may be another opening and is encouraging Jan to apply.

Imagine you are Jan and tell what you think might happen if you took the new job.

4. Imagine the following situations. Ask several of your classmates: What would you do if _____ ? How many different answers can you get?

a. You found a wallet with $50 in it and no identification.

b. You saw a friend of yours cheating on an exam.

c. Your friend asked you to do his homework for him.

d. You left the house in the morning and forgot your keys.

e. You lost your textbook and class notes the night before an important exam.

f. Your friend got sick all of a sudden.

g. You heard a strange noise in your house in the middle of the night.

h. You borrowed your friend's sweater and spilled ink on it.

i. You won first prize in a $500,000 lottery.

5. Tell about a trip you might make to a place that you know well.

> **EXAMPLE:** If I visit my friend in New York next fall, he will meet me at the airport. If his car is fixed, he will drive me to his parent's house.

6. Most of us will never have the time or money to travel to all the places that we would like to go to, but we sometimes like to imagine we could travel to far-off places that we have read or heard about. Imagine you have been given enough time and money to take a three-month trip to all the places you have dreamed of visiting. Give a short talk or write a short composition describing your imaginary trip.

7. Tell several things you would say in each of the following situations. Use the expression "If I were you," to give advice.

Situation a

A friend of yours is planning to drive home from a party and asks you to come along. You know that he has already had several drinks and is about to have another.

Situation b

Another friend tells you that he is going to buy a used car from a car dealer who advertises on television. You know that the ads are lies because last year you bought a car from the same dealer.

Situation c

A friend announces that she is going to take a course which you took last semester and didn't like.

Situation d

Another one of your friends, who has always been a very serious student, announces that he is going to quit school.

8. Describe a situation in which you gave advice to a friend. Did the friend accept your advice?

9. Either write a short composition or give a short talk about the birthday celebration you would have if you had the time and money to celebrate your next birthday in whatever way you wanted. Where would you celebrate? How many friends would you invite? What kind of food and drink would you serve? What kind of entertainment would you have? What gifts would you like to receive? Since the party is imaginary, there are no restrictions. You could, for example, hire a private plane and bring friends from all over the world.

10. Imagine you have been selected for a position of power: the leader of a country, the mayor of a city, the president or head of the school that you are now attending. Give a short talk or write a short composition telling about the changes you would make if you held one of these positions.

LESSON
10

STRUCTURE SKILLS
Past conditions using <u>if</u> (contrary to fact)

Wishes about past events (REVIEW)

Giving advice about future events using <u>should</u> (REVIEW)

Giving advice about past events using
<u>should</u> + <u>have</u> + past participle

Rick

Several years ago Rick met Sally and fell in love with her. Sally wanted to get married, but Rick wanted to go away to school first. He told Sally that they would get married when he came back. Rick asked his best friend, Mike, to see Sally from time to time so she wouldn't be lonely.

Last week, Rick received an announcement of Sally's marriage to Mike. It made him very unhappy because he still loves Sally and can't forget her. He can't make himself think about other girls.

EXERCISES

1. The story tells what really happened to Rick. If Rick, or Sally, or Mike had acted differently, other things might have happened. For example:

If Rick had never met Sally, he wouldn't have fallen in love with her.

Ask other students in class what they think might have happened:

    a. If Rick and Sally had gotten married

    b. If Sally had gone away to school

    c. If Rick had met another girl at school

    d. If Mike had really been a good friend

    e. If the wedding announcement had gotten lost in the mail

How many different answers did you get?

2. Rick is very unhappy. He is also angry at Sally and Mike. What do you think he wishes he could do?

    EXAMPLE: He wishes he could punch Mike in the nose.

3. *Role Play*: Rick is talking to his parents. He is asking them what he should do about Sally and Mike. (One student plays Rick; two other students play his mother and father.)

4. Everybody makes mistakes—big ones and little ones. Think about some things you have done in the past that you wish you hadn't done. Tell both the fact and your wish.

> EXAMPLES: I said something very unkind to my friend. (fact)
>
> I wish I hadn't said it.
>
> I stayed up too late last night. (fact)
>
> I wish I had gone to bed earlier.

5. Write a short composition or give a short talk about something you regret doing. Tell what you wish you had done.

6. Maybe you have thought about what life would have been like if you had been born in another century and in a different place. Choose another time and place for yourself and describe the life you would have led. For example, you might be a cowboy in the American West a hundred years ago. Or you might be a great painter at the time of the Italian Renaissance.

Vocabulary

Here are some adjectives used to describe people's personalities or characters. Look up the words you do not know in your dictionary and discuss their meanings with the class. Members of the class should try to make the meanings of each of the words clear by telling how a person described by each word would act.

> EXAMPLE: shy
>
> *A shy person is uncomfortable with strangers. He may be afraid to talk to people he does not know well.*

ambitious	patient
calm	polite
confident	serious
considerate	sincere
curious	stubborn
courageous	studious
friendly	talkative
generous	thoughtful
helpful	witty

Use some of the words listed on the preceding page to describe the personality of someone you know, or of a famous person in history whom you have read about. Tell about the person's life, giving examples of actions that show personality traits. You can either give a short talk or write a short composition about the person you have chosen.

11

STRUCTURE SKILLS
Must and have to to express necessity

The Life of a Student

During his first year in law school Roberto had to work very hard. His classes were very difficult and he wanted to get very good grades. He had to go the library every evening to study, and he had to get up early every weekday to attend class. On weekends he didn't have to go to class, but he still had to study. He usually didn't take the time to eat regular meals, so he had to eat candy bars and crackers for dinner.

By the end of the first semester Roberto wasn't feeling very well. He was always tired and often nervous. It was hard for him to concentrate on his studies. Roberto's friends were worried about him. His roommate told him that he had to see a doctor.

The doctor examined Roberto carefully. "You're basically healthy," he said, "but you have to take better care of yourself. You must get eight hours of sleep a night. You must eat three good meals every day, and you must not work so hard."

Roberto tried to follow the doctor's orders. He still studied hard, but he found that he didn't have to study in the library every evening. Once in a while he spent an evening relaxing and talking with his friends. He tried to get more sleep, and to eat better meals. After a month he felt much better. He also got good grades. Roberto found out that good students have to work hard, but they also have to take care of their health.

EXERCISES

1. Name five or more things that it is necessary for good students like Roberto to do. Use either *must* or *have to* in your sentences.

>   **EXAMPLE:** Good students must (have to)
>   study regularly.

2. Name five or more things that it is necessary for a good teacher to do.

> **EXAMPLE:** A good teacher must (has to)
> prepare his classes carefully.

3. Roberto's roommate gave a surprise party for Roberto at the end of the semester. The roommate had to plan the party carefully so that everything would be prepared, but Roberto would not know about it. Construct as many sentences as you can about what Roberto's roommate had to do before the party.

> **EXAMPLE:** He had to call all of Roberto's friends
> to invite them to the party.

4. Shirley is planning to take a trip to Mexico. Several weeks ago she made a list of all the things she had to do to get ready for her trip. Every time she did something on her list she crossed it out so that she would know that she didn't have to do it again. This is what Shirley's list looks like now:

~~Buy a new suitcase~~	Change dollars to pesos
Practice speaking Spanish	Buy two pairs of comfortable
~~Study map of Mexico~~	shoes
Get passport	~~Write hotel in Acapulco~~
~~Write cousins in Mexico City~~	Buy travelers checks
~~Buy a new raincoat~~	Pack suitcase
~~Read book about Mexican~~	Ask neighbor to water plants
~~history~~	Call friends to say good-by

It is not necessary for Shirley to do any of the things that are crossed off her list (because she has already done them).

> **EXAMPLE:** She doesn't have to buy a new suitcase.

Construct five more sentences about things that Shirley doesn't have to do.

It is still necessary for Shirley to do several things.

> **EXAMPLE:** She still must (has to) pack her suitcase.

Construct seven more sentences about things that Shirley still must (has to) do.

5. Before Ms. Liu could get her driver's license she had to take a test on the rules of the road. In order to remember the rules she made a list. Here is her list:

> Carry driver's license at all times
> Don't drive over 30 miles per hour in a residential zone
> Signal before turning or changing lanes
> Come to a complete stop at a red light
> Don't turn from the middle lane
> Use lights after dark
> Give pedestrians the right of way at crossings
> Don't pass another car on a hill
> Drive slowly near schools and hospitals
> Slow down when making turns

Use Ms. Liu's list of rules to construct sentences telling what drivers must (have to) do, and what they must not do.

EXAMPLES: Drivers must (have to) come to a complete stop at a red light.

Drivers must not drive over 30 miles an hour in a residential zone.

6. Linda is eight years old. Like many other children her age she is often mischievous. At home, she fights with her older brother and teases her younger sister. She doesn't behave well in school either. Linda's mother and Linda's teacher are always telling Linda that she must not misbehave.

Imagine you are Linda's mother. Tell Linda what she must not do at home.

EXAMPLE: Linda, you must not pull your sister's hair.

Now imagine that you are Linda's teacher. Tell Linda what she must not do at school.

EXAMPLE: Linda, you must not throw chalk at other students.

7. Both children and adults follow rules in their lives. These rules can be made by our parents, our teachers, the school administration, our bosses, the local government, the national government, and many other people or groups. Most people also make rules for themselves about what they must (have to) do or must not do. Write down five or more things that you must do or that you must not do. Talk about these with the class. If possible try to decide who made the rule, and who else the rule applies to. It may be helpful to put some of the answers on the blackboard for general discussion.

> **EXAMPLES:** I must (have to) have a current driver's license if I want to drive a car. (This rule is made by the government. It applies to all drivers.)
>
> I must not be late for class. (This rule is made by the teacher. It applies to all students.)
>
> I must (have to) wash my hair twice a week. (I made the rule. It applies only to myself.)

Vocabulary: Two-word verbs

Here are some more common two-word verbs and their meanings:

call off (cancel)	pass out (distribute)
fill out (complete)	pick out (select)
hand in (submit)	point out (indicate)
leave out (omit)	put off (postpone)
look over (examine)	turn down (reject)
look up (search for)	

Construct sentences with approximately the same meanings as the sentences given, using the appropriate form of a two-word verb. You will sometimes have to separate the parts of the verb.

> **EXAMPLE:** Roger knew that if he didn't pass the entrance exam the university would *reject him.*
>
> Roger knew that if he didn't pass the entrance exam the university would *turn him down.*

a. Roger had to *complete* an application form to take the university entrance exam.

b. Roger went to the bookstore to *select* the books he needed to study for the exam.

c. The night before the exam Roger was nervous. He wished the university would *cancel* the exam or *postpone it.*

d. At ten o'clock the next morning a teacher *distributed* the examination papers.

e. He *indicated* that the students should follow the directions carefully.

f. Students should not *omit* any questions.

g. They could not use a dictionary to *search for* words.

h. They should *examine* their papers carefully before *submitting them.*

STRUCTURE SKILLS
Must and might to express inferences

People Watching

Sarah and Anne are university students. After their morning classes they often meet at an inexpensive neighborhood restaurant to eat and chat about life at school. Sometimes instead of talking about school they play a game they call "people watching." They take turns looking at and listening to the people around them and making guesses about the people's lives.

Yesterday Anne started the game by observing the older woman at the next table. These were Anne's observations: "She has gray hair and a few wrinkles. She must be about forty-five years old. She smiles a lot. She must be kind. She is wearing a ring on her left hand. She must be married. She is not eating much for lunch. She might be on a diet. She is carrying a package from a toy store. She must have gone shopping this morning. She might have bought a present for her grandchild. It might be his birthday."

Sarah looked carefully at a man on the other side of the room. These were her observations: "He's eating a big lunch. He must be hungry. He's eating it very quickly. He must be in a hurry. He might be late for work. He looks tired. He must have worked hard this morning. He's tanned. He might work out of doors. Judging from his clothes, he might be a construction worker. They are building a new hospital a few blocks away. He might be one of the workers who are building it."

Of course, Sarah and Anne never really know if their guesses about people are true. But they usually have good reasons for thinking that they are. In any case, the game is fun.

EXERCISES

1. What guesses did Anne make about the woman at the next table? Which guesses did Anne believe were probably true? Which guesses was Anne less sure of?

2. What guesses did Sarah make about the man on the other side of the room? Which guesses did Sarah believe were probably true? Which guesses was Sarah less sure of?

3. How many different guesses can you make about the present or the future from the following information? (You believe that your guesses are probably correct.)

> EXAMPLE: Susan isn't eating much for lunch these days.
>
> *She must be on a diet. She must eat a big breakfast.*

a. Ellie is studying very hard this afternoon.

b. Blanca has a temperature of 101° F.*

c. Peter speaks English with a British accent.

d. George is carrying books in three different languages.

e. Roger went to get his passport this morning.

f. There are dark clouds in the sky.

g. Mr. Novak is running to catch the bus.

h. Tim just came in the door wearing a wet raincoat.

i. The book is listed in the library's card catalog, but I can't find it on the shelves.

j. Mike and Sam are in the same class.

4. How many different guesses can you make about present or future events from the following information? (This time you are less certain that your guesses are correct.)

> EXAMPLE: Rick isn't in school today.
>
> *He might be sick. He might be out of town.*

a. Takeko is looking at travel advertisements.

b. There are a few clouds in the sky.

c. Sally's forehead is a little warm.

d. I'm looking for a book by Ernest Hemingway. The library has some American novels.

* Normal temperature is 98.6° F.

e. Mike and Stavros go to the same school.

f. Ben always sits in the front of the classroom.

g. The baby is crying.

h. The dog next door is barking very loudly.

i. Piero looks very nervous.

j. Rick is reading a letter from his girlfriend.

5. Use the information below to make guesses about past events. Use *must have* if you believe that your guesses are probably correct and *might have* if you are less certain.

> **EXAMPLES:** When I looked out of the window this morning the sidewalk was very wet.
>
> *It must have rained last night.*
>
> Mike looks tired.
>
> *He might have studied very hard last night.*
> **or**
> *He might have gotten up early this morning.*

a. Susan has lost a lot of weight.

b. Chen just left the barber shop.

c. Paul's glasses are broken and his coat is dirty and torn.

d. The two thieves have just bought new clothes and a big, fast car.

e. The grass in Mr. Cohn's front yard has turned brown.

f. I saw Bobby's dog in the park this morning. Bobby wasn't there.

g. My watch says 10:00. The clock on the wall says 12:15.

h. The garage door is broken, and the new car is not there.

i. The test was very easy, but Peter failed it.

j. I never received a letter from my friend. He promised that he would write me.

6. Do some people watching on your own. Observe strangers in a restaurant, library, park, or another busy place. Tell the class about someone that you saw. Make some guesses about him or her.

13

STRUCTURE SKILLS
Present and past participles used as adjectives

Boris

Boris has starred in a dozen horror movies. He always plays a monster, a vampire, or some other frightening character. He uses a lot of make-up to make his face as horrifying as possible. Boris finds it interesting to play monsters. He has never been interested in playing romantic heroes, even though he is quite good-looking without his make-up.

Last year, after he had made five horror movies in a row, Boris was so exhausted that he wanted to take a long vacation. He went to a tropical island where no one knew him and he didn't have to do anything but lie on the beach. But soon he was bored. Lying on the beach all day with nothing to do can be boring. Boris wanted to do something interesting and exciting again. After that vacation Boris decided that he liked his exhausting schedule after all.

When he came back from his vacation, Boris began working on a new movie right away. He was so glad to be occupied again that he didn't think about being tired. All his attention was devoted to his performance. Boris was determined to be more frightening in this movie than he had ever been before.

In real life Boris isn't frightening at all. People are always amazed to see how handsome he is off the screen. He is also very kind, especially with children. That is why Boris was so surprised last week when a little girl he met on the street screamed and ran away from him. Boris had forgotten to take off his make-up.

EXERCISES

1. Tell the class about some things or experiences you think are interesting. List five or more of these on a sheet of paper.

    EXAMPLES: I think horror movies are interesting.

        For me, learning a language is interesting.

2. Exchange lists with one of your classmates. Do the two of you agree on your choices? Working together, write a new list that shows how you both feel.

> EXAMPLES: Both Carlos and I think classical music
> is interesting.
>
> Carlos thinks football games are interesting,
> but I think they are very boring.

3. Here are some additional sets of present and past participles that can be used as adjectives. Construct a sentence for each word.

annoying	annoyed
astonishing	astonished
alarming	alarmed
confusing	confused
charming	charmed
embarrassing	embarrassed
exciting	excited
pleasing	pleased
relaxing	relaxed
surprising	surprised
tiring	tired

4. Can you think of an experience that frightened you very much when you were a child? Write or tell about your frightening experience. Does it seem as frightening now as it did in the past?

5. Can you think of a time when you or someone you know was very surprised by something? What was so surprising?

6. Either give a short talk or write a short composition titled "The Most Interesting Person I Have Ever Met."

Vocabulary: Occupations
Can you give a short description of each of the following occupations?

architect	beautician
journalist	housekeeper
housewife	social worker

See how many other occupations you and your classmates can name. Write them on the board. Give one or two sentence descriptions of each occupation.

EXAMPLE: An architect draws plans for buildings.

If an English language newspaper is available, look at some of the advertisements for jobs. Which occupations are mentioned?

LESSON
14

STRUCTURE SKILLS
Some ways of expressing cause (<u>because</u>, <u>because of</u>)
and concession (<u>although</u>, <u>in spite of</u>)

Lana

Lana is now making her tenth movie. It will probably be as successful as all the others she has made. Lana can't act, sing, or dance, but she is beautiful and very sexy. None of her fellow actors like her, but the head of the movie studio does.

Lana never comes to the movie studio on time. When she was making her last movie, the producer sent a driver to her house every morning to bring her to the studio. But Lana was still late. All the other actors had to wait. Lana never tries to memorize her lines before she comes to work. When the cameras start to turn, Lana tries to remember what she is supposed to say. She often says the wrong line.

No actor wants to make a movie with Lana. Everyone knows that she is difficult to work with. Nevertheless, movie studios all over the world keep on asking her to star in their movies. Why? Because Lana's movies are always popular. Millions of people go to see them. Nobody likes Lana in real life, but they love her in the movies.

EXERCISES

1. Complete the following sentences by adding a clause (a group of words containing both a subject and a verb).

    a. Lana makes a lot of movies although _____she can't act_____ .

    b. Everyone has to wait for Lana because ___she is always late___ .

    c. None of Lana's fellow actors like her because _____ .

    d. Lana often says the wrong line because _____ .

    e. Movie studios keep on asking Lana to make movies because

    _____ .

    f. Movie studios keep on asking Lana to make movies although

    _____ .

    g. Millions of people go to see Lana's movies because

    _____ .

h. Millions   of   people   go   to   see   Lana's   movies   although

_____ .

i. Nobody likes Lana in real life because _____ .

2. This time complete the sentences by adding a noun phrase only (no verb).

a. Lana makes a lot of movies in spite of __her poor acting__ .

b. Everyone has to wait for Lana because of __her lateness__ .

c. None of Lana's fellow actors like her because of _____ .

d. Lana often says the wrong line because of _____ .

e. Movie studios keep on asking Lana to make movies because of

_____ .

f. Movie studios keep on asking Lana to make movies in spite of

_____ .

g. Millions   of   people   go   to   see   Lana's   movies   because   of

_____ .

h. Millions   of   people   go   to   see   Lana's   movies   in   spite   of

_____ .

i. Nobody likes Lana in real life because of _____ .

3. In the United States people do most of their shopping in large supermarkets, although they may occasionally buy a few things in small neighborhood grocery stores. Each kind of shopping has advantages and disadvantages:

Supermarket	**Small grocery stores**
Large selection of merchandise	Smaller selection of merchandise
Faster	Takes more time (may have to go to more than one store)
Free parking near store	Often no parking space provided
Prices usually lower	Prices a bit higher
Impersonal and boring	Friendly (can chat with owner)
Must pay for delivery	Free delivery to regular customers
One mile away (need car)	Down the street (can walk)

Construct ten sentences about shopping in the United States using the words *because* (*because of*) or *although* (*in spite of*).

> **EXAMPLES:** Americans like to shop in supermarkets *because there is a large selection of merchandise.*
>
> **or**
>
> *because of the large selection of merchandise.*
>
>
> Americans may occasionally shop in a small grocery store, *although the prices are higher.*
>
> **or**
>
> *in spite of the higher prices.*

Do supermarkets exist in your country? Are they usual or unusual? Do they have any advantages? Disadvantages?

4. Make a list similar to that found in Exercise 3 of the advantages and disadvantages of living in a large city versus living in a small town. After you have completed your list, use it to construct sentences with the expressions *because* (*because of*) and *although* (*in spite of*).

5. Use the method of Exercises 4 and 5 to either give a short talk or write a short composition about the advantages and disadvantages of two places or activities you know well:

a small school	vs.	a large school
living in a house	vs.	living in an apartment
an active vacation	vs.	a restful vacation

(or a subject of your choice)

LESSON

15

STRUCTURE SKILLS
Comparisons of equality and inequality

The Big Apple

When Liz first moved to New York City a few years ago she didn't like it at all. She had grown up in a small town and the city was full of unpleasant surprises. Her home town was quiet. The only noise she was used to hearing in the morning was the sound of birds singing. When she looked up she saw the sky. In New York tall buildings almost hid the sky, and she was awakened to the sound of the honking of cars' horns and the screeching of their tires.

In her home town Liz knew almost everyone. New York had lots of people but all of them were strangers. Many of them didn't seem very friendly.

Liz's home town was clean, but the streets in New York were always dirty. People threw trash on the streets and didn't seem to care. The subway was dirty too. The first time Liz rode the subway she was terrified by the noise and the crowds. People told her not to ride the subway at night because it was dangerous. Her first night in New York Liz stayed in her room and cried.

After a few weeks Liz began to make friends, and she also began to see the city in a different way. She met people from all over the world who had come to make a new life for themselves in New York, as she had done. Many of the people she met were more interesting than the people in her home town.

Liz also became aware of many new things to do in a large city. She could go to a different movie or concert every night, and some of them were free. In little restaurants near her apartment she could try food from a dozen different countries. All kinds of wonderful things were on sale in the stores. Of course Liz couldn't afford to buy everything she saw, but even window shopping in New York was fun. Although she still thought that the New York subway was noisy and dirty, she found out that it could take her anywhere in the city she wanted to go.

Liz hasn't forgotten the good things in her home town, but by now she has decided that she likes New York too. It is full of excitment and opportunity. Now she knows why people call New York City "The Big Apple."

EXERCISES

1. One evening Liz wrote a list of the differences between life in New York and life in her home town. Construct five or more sentences that Liz might have written, using adjectives to make your comparisons.

> EXAMPLES: The buildings in New York are taller
> than the buildings in my home town.
>
> The people in New York are more interesting
> than the people in my home town.

2. Construct five more sentences that Liz might have written, using nouns to make your comparisons.

> EXAMPLE: There are more people in New York than in my home town.

3. After she had lived in New York for three months, Liz wrote a letter to her uncle comparing the big city with her home town. The letter began:

Dear Uncle Bob,

When I first came to New York I thought the city was terrible, but now I like it very much. However, New York is very different from our town.

Finish Liz's letter. (Students can either write their own endings to the letter and then share them with the class, or the letter can be written collectively with one student writing the responses on the blackboard.)

4. Many of your fellow students have lived in more than one place. Prepare as many questions as you can for interviews with classmates comparing two different places they know. For example, you might ask which place is larger in area, is more densely populated, is more expensive to live in, has better public transportation, has more interesting cultural events.

Students may volunteer to be interviewed by the entire class, or interviews can be conducted in pairs or small groups. The students being interviewed should explain and add details to their answers.

5. Use the questions you prepared for Exercise 4 to compare your home town with another place you have visited or lived in. Explain your answers.

6. Peggy and Pat are sisters. People are always telling them that they look very much alike. Peggy and Pat agree that they look alike, but they also think that in some ways they are very different.

Peggy	**Pat**
Has blue eyes	Has blue eyes
Has long, light brown hair	Has long, dark brown hair
Is five feet, four inches tall	Is five feet, three inches tall
Is twenty-two years old	Is twenty-four years old
Likes to wear casual clothes	Likes to wear conservative clothes
Likes large parties	Likes to spend the evening with a few good friends
Completed high school	Graduated from college
Drives a large car	Drives a small car

Construct sentences comparing Peggy and Pat. Tell the ways in which they are alike and the ways in which they are different.

> **EXAMPLES:** Peggy has the same color eyes as Pat.
>
> Peggy's hair is longer than Pat's.

7. George and Jerry answered an advertisement for the same job: assistant manager of a bank in a small city. The manager of the bank interviewed each of them and received letters of recommendation from their previous employers. Then he considered the information he had gathered:

George Watson—Age: 35; married, two children (aged 10 and 12). Education: B.A. in economics; master's degree in accounting. Has worked at the Central Bank in his home town since graduating from college. Has received one promotion and is now an assistant manager. Is considered a steady and reliable worker. Hasn't missed a day's work in ten years.

Jerry Gordon—Age: 28; divorced, one child (aged 3). Education: B.A. in English literature (honors student); master's degree in business administration. Worked at the National Bank of New York City for two years; was promoted twice. Left to travel around the world for six months. Then was appointed vice president of a small new bank in Boston. His department specialized in home mortgage loans for young couples who could not get loans at other banks. He was considered an innovative worker; brought many new ideas to his work. Left Boston because he no longer wants to live in a large city. Presently unemployed.

Compare the two applicants for the job. Which one do you think the bank manager decided to hire? Why? Would you come to the same decision, if you were the manager? Which man do you think would be more interesting to talk to?

8. Give a short talk or write a short composition comparing two different experiences you know well. Here are some possibilities:

Living in a house/living in an apartment

Studying in a small school/studying in a large school

Working during the day/working at night

Working full-time/working part-time

An active vacation/a relaxing vacation

Attending a large party and meeting new people/attending a small party with close friends

Listening to classical music/listening to popular music

Watching television/going to the movies

Learning a language by talking to people/learning a language by reading

Vocabulary: Adverbs
Many adverbs are formed by adding -*ly* to adjectives:

efficient   efficiently

Following is a list of adjectives modifying nouns. Construct sentences in which adverbs modify verbs.

EXAMPLE: an efficient worker

The new secretary works efficiently.

a graceful dancer	an awkward runner
a forceful speaker	a nervous speaker
an accurate typist	a clever worker
a rapid reader	an anxious listener
a careless writer	a cautious driver

LESSON
16

STRUCTURE SKILLS
Superlatives

Review of comparatives

Max

Max owns a large ranch in Texas, a large state in the southwestern part of the United States. Like other Texans, Max loves to boast. As soon as he meets people, Max starts to tell them about how wonderful his ranch is. No one else can get a word in edgewise. Max says that his ranch is the most beautiful place on earth. It has the most spectacular sunsets. At sundown the sky is the reddest anyone has ever seen.

Right after Max is finished talking about his ranch, he takes out pictures of his wife and children. Max tells everyone that his wife is the most beautiful woman in Texas, and the best cook in the United States. His children are the smartest children that have ever been born. Max will go on for hours talking about his family. Some people get very tired of listening to him.

The other day Max was driving his big car along an empty road. He was very thirsty and he stopped at a small farm for a drink of water. When the old farmer came out of his little house, Max asked, "What do you do on this little place?"

"I raise chickens," said the farmer.

"How large is your property?"

"Not very big," said the farmer, "about fifty feet in front and maybe a hundred feet long, but I have as much space as I need."

"You should see my place," boasted Max. "When I get into my car at 9:00 a.m. I drive and I drive and I drive and I still don't reach the end of my property until six o'clock that night."

"I know," said the farmer. "I once had a car like that."

EXERCISES

1. Max is always boasting. He tells people that his ranch is the biggest and the best ranch in the world. What else does Max boast about in the story?

Can you imagine some other things Max might boast about that are not mentioned in the story?

Here is some information about the cars that Max, Max's wife, and the farmer drive.

	Max's Car	Wife's Car	Farmer's Car
Length	18'2"	16'6"	13'3"
Weight	5,000 lbs.	3,800 lbs.	2,600 lbs.
Cost	$18,600	$12,300	$2,000
Model year	1981	1979	1963
Fastest speed	120 mph	100 mph	60 mph
Number of miles driven	6,600	18,700	80,900
Miles per gallon of gas	8	12	20

Abbreviations used in chart: ' = feet, " = inches, lbs. = pounds, mph = miles per hour

2. Compare two cars—Max's car and his wife's car—by answering the following questions. Answer in complete sentences.

> **EXAMPLE:** Which car is heavier?
>
> *Max's car is heavier than his wife's car.*

a. Which car is lighter?

b. Which car is older?

c. Which car is shorter?

d. Which car is longer?

e. Which car has been driven more miles?

f. Which car uses more gasoline?

g. Which car is faster?

h. Which car was more expensive to buy?

i. Which car was less expensive to buy?

j. Which car is more expensive to run?

3. Now compare Max's wife's car with the farmer's car. Use the same questions as in Exercise 2.

4. This time compare Max's car with the farmer's car. Again use the questions from Exercise 2.

5. This time compare all three cars by answering the following questions. Answer in complete sentences.

> **EXAMPLE:** Which car is the heaviest of the three?
>
> *Max's car is the heaviest of the three.*

a. Which car is the lightest?

b. Which car is the oldest?

c. Which car is the shortest?

d. Which car is the longest?

e. Which car has been driven the most miles?

f. Which car uses the most gasoline?

g. Which car is the fastest?

h. Which car was the most expensive to buy?

i. Which car was the least expensive to buy?

j. Which car is the most expensive to run?

k. Which car travels the most miles on ten gallons of gas?

6. Students should take turns asking another student one of the following questions.

> What is the largest city in your country?
>
> What is the largest city you have ever seen?
>
> What is the largest city in the world?
>
> What is the most interesting place to visit in your home town?
>
> What is the most interesting place to visit in your country?
>
> What is the most interesting place you have ever visited?

After this exercise is completed, students can try to construct their own questions. Questions could be about: the longest river, the highest mountain, the most beautiful city, the most famous movie star, the most exciting book, the best athlete.

7. The class should divide into groups of three. Each student in the group writes his or her name in one of the spaces on the top line of the chart below and fills in the necessary information in the column underneath.

Name			
Height			
Age			
Number of persons in family			
Number of letters in first name			

After each group has filled in its chart, students should use the information to construct sentences comparing any two students in the group or comparing one person with the others.

EXAMPLES: Enrique is taller than Maria.

Mohammed is taller than Enrique.

Mohammed is the tallest of the three.

TWO

PROBLEM-SOLVING EXERCISES

Moving to Another City

The Thompson family lives in a large city in the Midwest. They all like city life for a number of reasons. It is easy for them to see new plays and movies and to go to concerts and sporting events. They enjoy shopping in the large department stores. Because they have lived in their house for a long time, they have made many friends in the neighborhood.

Both parents work; the two children attend a nearby high school. The father is an engineer; the mother is a school teacher. They are both paid quite well, but the father's job has become very boring. Also, it doesn't offer much chance for advancement.

Yesterday the father received a long-distance phone call offering him a new job in a small town a thousand miles away. The pay would be a little better, but the most important thing is that the job would be much more interesting. He could do important research and maybe be head of a department after a few years. The new job seems very attractive even though it means moving the family away from their home.

The problem is that no one else in the family wants to move. They will miss their friends. They will miss the excitement of city life. Also, because teaching jobs are hard to find, the mother will probably not be able to find a job right away.

Decide the best thing for the family to do and give the reasons for your decision. Think about the advantages and disadvantages for each member of the family.

The family should move. _____

The family should stay. _____

Reasons _____

_____

QUESTIONS FOR DISCUSSION

1. In the story about the Thompsons, it is the father who is offered a new job in a different city. What if Mrs. Thompson, the mother, were offered the new job? Would your answer to the question "Should the family move?" be different? If so, why?

2. Imagine you could move to any place in the world you wanted. What place would you choose? What things would influence your choice: availability of jobs, being near to friends and family, cultural and recreational opportunities, climate, etc.?

Judging Movies

Last week you were elected a member of the committee that judges all new movies and decides who should be allowed to see them. It is your job to rate five different movies each week. This is the rating system you should use:

G   General (anyone may see it)

PG   Parental Guidance (anyone may enter the theater, but parents are warned that the movie may not be suitable for small children)

R   Restricted (Children under 17 may see the movie only if they are with an adult)

X   Adults only

These are descriptions of the movies you will see. Circle your rating and be prepared to tell why you made your choice.

Movie 1
This is a comedy about a children's baseball team. The team's coach is really a nice man, but he drinks a lot and uses bad language.

    Your rating: G   PG   R   X

Movie 2
This movie contains several violent scenes showing swimmers torn apart by a shark. It is very exciting, and some parts are funny. There is no bad language.

    Your rating: G   PG   R   X

Movie 3
This is a dramatic film about the American West. The hero is a tough old cavalry officer who leads an attack on an Indian village. Although there are no violent scenes, it is evident that several Indian women and

children are killed in the battle. At the end of the movie the cavalrymen celebrate their victory over the Indians.

Your rating: G   PG   R   X

Movie 4

This movie takes place during wartime. The director has included several extremely violent, realistic battle scenes in order to show that all wars are immoral.

Your rating: G   PG   R   X

Movie 5

This is a movie about the attempted murder of a young and beautiful girl by her jealous stepmother. The girl does not die because the servant who is supposed to cut out her heart with a knife takes pity on her and lets her go. Later, the stepmother learns that the girl is still alive and again tries to kill her. The movie is an animated cartoon based on a famous story which has been told to children for over a hundred years.

Your rating: G   PG   R   X

QUESTIONS FOR DISCUSSION

1. Compare your ratings with those of other students. The teacher can show the numbers of students selecting each rating on the blackboard. Two students whose ratings of the same movie differ may want to debate the reason for their choices.

2. Movie 4 shows violent action but tries to teach that such action is wrong. Movie 3 does not show violence but seems to approve of it. Do you think it is important to rate movies only by what they show, or should the moral attitude of the film influence your ratings?

3. Many Americans are concerned about their children seeing so much violence in movies and on TV. Some people believe that children who grow up seeing such violence will learn to do violent things themselves. Other people argue that children have always been told violent stories and it doesn't seem to hurt them. What do you think? Are children in the country where you grew up told stories or folktales that deal with violent events?

4. Imagine you have been asked to take care of the twelve-year-old daughter of a friend for the afternoon. You decide to take her to the movies. What kind of movie would you choose? You may describe an actual movie you have seen, or an imaginary one.

The Marriage Proposal

Both Tim and Maria are students attending university in a foreign country. Tim is twenty-five, and Maria is a few years younger. Two years ago they met through a mutual friend. They liked each other immediately, although their backgrounds are very different. They come from different countries and are used to different customs and religions. Tim's family is extremely wealthy and is very important in his country. Maria's family is not rich. In fact, her family had to struggle to send her to the university.

In spite of their differences, Tim and Maria really enjoy each other's company. They have many interests in common. They both enjoy music, they play the same sports, and they have many of the same friends. They laugh a lot together and seldom argue.

A few months ago, Tim realized that he was in love with Maria and would like to marry her. He thinks that she would accept his proposal of marriage, but he is afraid that his parents will not approve because of the differences in his and Maria's backgrounds. Tim is very fond of his parents, and their approval is important to him. Tim and his family had always thought that he would return home after he had completed school and help his father to manage the family business. Tim is afraid that Maria would not be happy living so close to his parents, and that she and her parents would be unhappy if she lived far away from them permanently.

What should Tim and Maria do?

A. They should not get married. The differences in their backgrounds would prevent their marriage from being successful. _____

B. They should marry and return to Tim's home town. Tim's parents would probably accept Maria after a while. _____

C. They should get married but live in Maria's country. _____

D. Another solution _____

_____

Be ready to give reasons for your answer. Think about the advantages and disadvantages of each solution for Tim, Maria, Tim's parents, and Maria's parents.

QUESTIONS FOR DISCUSSION

1. In your opinion, which of the following are important to consider in choosing someone as a marriage partner?

   a. Physical attraction

   b. Common interests

   c. Similar family background

   d. Common national culture

   e. Similar religious beliefs

   f. Ability to enjoy each other's company

   g. Potential to be a good parent

   h. Other factors

   _____

   _____

2. In the country where you grew up, or in another country you know well, how do most people meet their future husbands or wives?

   a. People meet each other informally at work or at school.

   b. Couples are formally introduced to each other by mutual friends.

   c. Possible marriage partners are formally introduced to each other by parents or relatives. The couple decides whether or not to get married.

   d. Marriages are arranged by parents or relatives. The couple has little choice.

   e. Marriages are arranged by a marriage broker.

Have marriage customs where you grew up changed in recent times? If so, what were the customs of earlier times? When did these customs change?

Do you know how your parents met each other? Your grandparents?

3. In many countries the number of divorces has increased in recent decades. Several reasons have been given to explain this increase. Some people say that any increase in divorce is a sign of lowered moral standards. Others say that increases in the divorce rate may not be a sign of moral decay, but may simply mean that people are no longer forced to continue extremely unhappy marriages for the sake of society. What do you think?

What is the attitude toward divorced people where you grew up, or in other countries you know about? Are divorced people disapproved of, or are they treated just like anyone else? Is there a difference in attitudes toward divorced women and divorced men?

An Important Decision

Ellie is twenty-two and is studying to be an architect. She will graduate soon and has already sent out several applications for jobs in various parts of the country. Two architectural firms have offered her jobs.

The first offer she received was from a large and busy firm in New York City. It promised an excellent salary for a beginner and good benefits. The company has a reputation for treating its employees well. People tend to work there for a long time.

Ellie wouldn't mind the move to another city but she is concerned that her work there would not be very interesting. The firm has designed the same kinds of big buildings for many years and is not known for its originality. Furthermore, the young architects they hire usually must spend several years working on details of other architects' plans. Only after many years do they get to design their own buildings.

Ellie's other job offer comes from a group of friends of hers who have recently graduated from architectural school and have set up their own small office near her home. Ellie admires the quality of the work her friends have done. They are open to experiments in architectural design. Whenever possible they do work that will benefit people. The first job they did was to design a low-income housing project that would use solar energy. Since the firm is small, everyone participates in contributing new ideas.

This new firm, however, has not been able to make much money so far. Ellie would have a very small starting salary, just enough to live on. If the firm is not successful, she would lose her job after a few months.

Which job should Ellie take? Be prepared to give reasons for your answer.

_____ She should take the job with the large architectural firm.

_____ She should take the job with the small firm.

QUESTIONS FOR DISCUSSION

1. What do you consider important in choosing a job for yourself? In the following list of job advantages, which are very important to you, quite important, not important?

good pay

benefits

security

a chance for advancement to a better job

opportunity to do interesting work

opportunity to learn

a chance to meet interesting people

long vacations

other advantages that are important to you

_____

_____

_____

Do you think you would answer the question in the same way ten years from now, or might other advantages be more important?

2. If you have worked, describe to the class a job you have done. What were the advantages and disadvantages of the job? If you have not yet had a job, describe a friend's or relative's job.

3. What kind of job would you like to do in the future? What preparation or training do you need for that job?

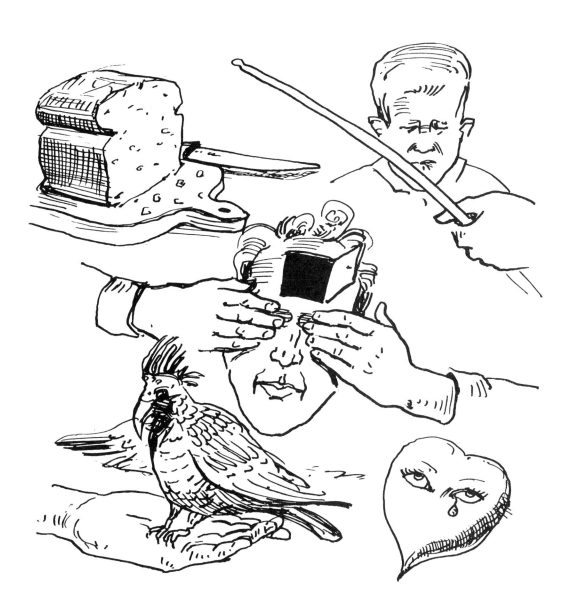

Proverbs

Here are some proverbs that many English speakers know.

A bird in the hand is worth two in the bush.
People who live in glass houses shouldn't throw stones.
Absence makes the heart grow fonder.
Out of sight, out of mind.
Birds of a feather flock together.
One man's meat is another man's poison.
Better late than never.
A stitch in time saves nine.
Half a loaf is better than none.
Spare the rod and spoil the child.

Proverbs may seen to be about one thing but may actually mean something else. For example, the first proverb seems to be about birds and bushes. However, this is not really what the proverb is about. The real meaning would be something like: It is better to have secure possession of something of lesser value, than to have only the promise of something of greater value.

QUESTIONS FOR DISCUSSION

1. Discuss in small groups and then with the whole class what you believe to be the real meaning of each of the proverbs. (It may be a good idea to discuss some of the difficult vocabulary first, with the teacher's help.)

2. Every language has its own proverbs. Each member of the groups should write down two or three proverbs in his or her own language and attempt to translate them into English. Proverbs are difficult to translate. If you are not sure your translation is good English, perhaps other students or the teacher can help discover the best translation.

3. Are there proverbs in your language that are the same as the English proverbs in this lesson? Do you have proverbs with the same meanings expressed in different ways? For example, "A bear in a trap is worth two bears in the forest" has the same meaning as "A bird in the hand is worth two in the bush," although the words are different.

4. Can you think of a situation in which you might use each of the proverbs that has been discussed in class? For example, if a friend of yours is trying to decide whether she should accept a good job now or wait to see if an even better job is offered to her in the future, you might advise her to take the job she is certain of by saying, "A bird in the hand is worth two in the bush."

5. Which proverbs do you think are true? Which offer good advice about how to live? Discuss your opinions with the class.

6. The third and fourth proverbs listed at the beginning of the lesson have opposite meanings. Which one do more people in the class think is true? Take a vote.

7. Do most of the proverbs you know give conservative advice, or do they advise people to change things?

8. In the culture in which you were raised, who is more likely to use proverbs, old people or young people? Men or women? (You might mention some other social customs or traditions that would help to explain your answer.)

THREE

MINI-GRAMMARS

Forming Negative Sentences

I. Forming negative sentences by adding <u>not</u> (n't)

If the affirmative (yes) sentence contains one of these words (forms of the verb *be*):

am   are   is   was   were

or one of these words (modal auxiliaries):

will   would   can   could   may   might   shall   should   must

add *not* after the word to make the sentence negative. In most speech and in informal writing *not* is shortened to *n't*.*

Affirmative	**Negative**
She is an engineer.	She isn't an engineer.
They were walking home last night.	They weren't walking home last night.
Who can swim?	Who can't swim?
She could have seen him.	She couldn't have seen him.
It will rain this afternoon.	It won't rain this afternoon.

If the affirmative sentence contains one of these words (forms of the verb *have*):

have   has   had

---

* See Appendix I for a list of shortened forms.

as the first auxiliary verb, add *not* (*n't*) to the word to make the sentence negative.

Affirmative	**Negative**
I have been wrong.	I haven't been wrong.
He has gone home.	He hasn't gone home.
We have been studying.	We haven't been studying.

When *have, has,* or *had* is the main verb in the affirmative sentence, speakers of British English often form the negative sentence by adding *not* (*n't*).

Affirmative	**Negative**
They have a car.	They haven't a car.

Speakers of American English usually say, "They don't have a car." Both forms are correct.*

II. Making sentences negative by adding <u>do not (don't)</u>, <u>does not</u> (doesn't), or <u>did not (didn't)</u>

When the affirmative sentence does not contain any of the words printed inside the boxes in the preceding section of this mini-grammar, add the words *does not* (*doesn't*), *do not* (*don't*), or *did not* (*didn't*) before the main verb in order to make the sentence negative. The main verb is then put in the simple form.†

Affirmative	**Negative**
He sings loudly.	He doesn't sing loudly.
They study hard.	They don't study hard.
Susan told a joke.	Susan didn't tell a joke.
They had a good time.	They didn't have a good time.

---

* Speakers of both British and American English also use a more informal expression: "They haven't got a car."

† The simple form (sometimes called the base form, the infinitive, or the dictionary form) is the same as the first person singular present for all English verbs except the verb *be*.

First pers. sing. pres.	*Simple form*
I walk	walk
I study	study
I go	go
I am	be

Does not (*doesn't*) is used for the present tense when the subject of the sentence is *he, she,* or *it,* or a word that one of these pronouns can replace (*Susan = she, the boy = he, my mother's cat = it*).

Do not (*don't*) is used for all other subjects in the present tense.

Did not (*didn't*) is used for all subjects in the past tense.

EXERCISES

Change the following affirmative sentences to negative sentences by adding *n't, doesn't, don't,* or *didn't* in the correct place. In some cases you will have to put the main verb in simple form.

> **EXAMPLES:** He was wearing a green shirt yesterday.
>
> *He wasn't wearing a green shirt yesterday.*
>
> She likes big parties.
>
> *She doesn't like big parties.*

1. The Thompsons like to give parties.

2. They have a lot of friends.

3. They gave several big parties last year.

4. Their parties are fun.

5. They serve a lot of good things to eat and drink.

6. Their guests bring things to contribute to the party.

7. The party tonight is going to be a success.

8. The guests are eating, dancing, and singing.

9. All the guests will have arrived by nine o'clock.

10. The party should be over by midnight.

11. The Thompsons enjoy their own parties.

12. They will give another party soon.

Forming Questions

You will notice that the rules for forming questions are similar in many ways to the rules given in Mini-grammar 1 for making sentences negative.

I. Forming questions by moving the first auxiliary verb

If the sentence contains one of these words (forms of the verb *be*):

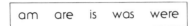

am   are   is   was   were

or one of these words (modal auxiliaries):

will   would   can   could   may   might   shall   should   must

move the word in front of the subject to form a question.

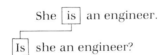

She $\boxed{\text{is}}$ an engineer.

$\boxed{\text{Is}}$ she an engineer?

Statement	**Question**
All the children were walking home.	Were all the children walking home?
Tommy can swim.	Can Tommy swim?

If the sentence contains one of these words (forms of the verb *have*):

have   has   had

as the first auxiliary verb, also move the word in front of the subject to form a question.

Statement	**Question**
I have been wrong.	Have I been wrong?

When *have, has,* or *had* is the main verb in the sentence, speakers of British English often form questions by moving it in front of the subject:

Statement   **Question**
He has a car.   Has he a car?

Speakers of American English usually say, "Does he have a car?" Both forms are correct.*

II. Forming questions with <u>does</u>, <u>do</u>, or <u>did</u>

When the statement does not contain any of the words in the boxes in the preceding section, questions are formed by putting *does, do,* or *did* in front of the subject. The main verb is put in the simple form.

Statement   **Question**
He sings loudly.   Does he sing loudly?

They study hard.   Do they study hard?

Susan told a joke.   Did Susan tell a joke?

They had a good time.   Did they have a good
                                       time?

Does is used for the present tense when the subject of the sentences is *he, she,* or *it,* or a word that one of these pronouns can replace (*Susan = she, the boy = he, my mother's cat = it*).
     Do is used for all other subjects in the present tense.
     Did is used for all subjects in the past tense.

EXERCISES

Change the statements in the exercises on page 93 (in Mini-grammar 1) to questions.

> EXAMPLES: He was wearing a green shirt yesterday. (affirmative statement)
>
> He wasn't wearing a green shirt yesterday. (negative statement)
>
> *Was he wearing a green shirt yesterday?* (question)

* Speakers of both British and American English also use a more informal expression: "He hasn't got a car."

She likes big parties. (affirmative statement)

She doesn't like big parties. (negative statement)

Does she like big parties? (question)

III. Forming questions that ask for particular information

The questions we have been talking about so far can all be answered *yes* or *no*. Another kind of question asks for a particular piece of information and requires a word or phrase like *who, what, why, where, when, whose, how,* or *how much* at the beginning of the question.*

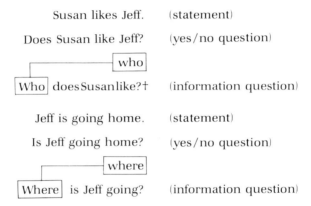

Susan likes Jeff.   (statement)

Does Susan like Jeff?   (yes/no question)

Who does Susan like?†   (information question)

Jeff is going home.   (statement)

Is Jeff going home?   (yes/no question)

Where is Jeff going?   (information question)

However, when the information asked for refers to the subject of the sentence, the question word replaces the subject and normal word order is retained.

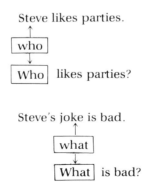

Steve likes parties.

Who likes parties?

Steve's joke is bad.

What is bad?

---

* Sometimes these are called *wh*-questions because all the question words (with the exception of *how*) begin with the letters *wh*.

† Formal English uses *whom*: "Whom does Susan like?"

EXERCISES

From the following statements form questions that ask for particular information.

EXAMPLE: Tommy's mother gave him some candy.

	Answers
What *did Tommy's mother give him?*	some candy
Who *gave Tommy the candy?*	his mother
Who *did she give the candy to?**	Tommy

1. Tommy will see his aunt tomorrow.

		Answers
Who _____	?	Tommy
Who(m) _____	?	his aunt
When _____	?	tomorrow

2. Tommy's aunt bought a dress last week that cost $50.

		Answers
Who _____	?	Tommy's aunt
What _____	?	a dress
How much _____	?	$50
When _____	?	last week

3. Tommy's cat sleeps on Tommy's bed in the morning.

		Answers
Who _____	?	Tommy's cat
Whose _____	?	Tommy's
Where _____	?	on Tommy's bed
When _____	?	in the morning

* Formal English: *Whom did she give the candy to?* or *To whom did she give the candy?*

Ways of Talking about Future Time

I. Common ways of talking about future events

English uses several different ways to talk about future events. Here are some of the most common:

    1. *will* + simple form*

        The plane will arrive.

    2. (*is, am, are*) + *going to* + verb

        The plane is going to arrive.

    3. *will* + *be* + verb + *-ing**

        The plane will be arriving.

The present tenses can also be used to talk about future events. Usually there is another word in the sentence to indicate the future (tomorrow, next week, 1988).

    4. simple present tense

        The plane arrives tomorrow morning.

    5. present progressive tense: (*is, am, are*) + verb + *-ing*

        The plane is arriving tomorrow morning.

In some cases any one of the ways of talking about future time may be used with little or no difference in meaning. In other cases there will be a subtle difference in meaning, or some forms will not be used.

* Some speakers of English use *shall* instead of *will* after *I* and *we*. Both forms are correct.

EXERCISES

These are some of the things Anne does every weekday morning. Use either *will* + verb or *is going to* + verb to tell what she will do next Tuesday.

> **EXAMPLE:** Anne wakes up at 6:15.
>
> Next Tuesday, *she will wake up at 6:15.*
> **or**
> Next Tuesday, *she is going to wake up at 6:15.*

1. Anne doesn't get up right away. Next Tuesday, _____ .

2. She lies in bed for fifteen minutes. Next Tuesday, _____ .

3. She gets up at 6:30. Next Tuesday, _____ .

4. She brushes her teeth. Next Tuesday, _____ .

5. She always forgets to put the cap back on the toothpaste.
Next Tuesday, _____ .

6. She doesn't get dressed right away. Next Tuesday, _____ .

7. She puts on her bathrobe. Next Tuesday, _____ .

8. She starts the coffee and puts the toast in the toaster.
Next Tuesday, _____ .

9. She looks over her notes for class while she eats breakfast.
Next Tuesday, _____ .

10. She looks forward to the next semester when she won't sign up for any
8:00 classes. Next Tuesday, _____ .

II. The future perfect tense

There is still another way of talking about events in the future. The future perfect tense consists of:

$$will + have + \text{past participle}^*$$

*Some English speakers use *shall* (rather than *will*) after *I* and *we*.

The future perfect is used to indicate a future event that will be completed sometime before another event in the future, or before a particular time in the future.

Hurry up! By the time we get to the party, all the food will have been eaten.

By the year 2000, we will have used up many of our natural resources.

By next week, the bookstore will have ordered all the books needed for next semester's classes.

EXERCISES

Complete the following sentences by telling what you or someone else will have done before the time mentioned:

1. By the end of this week, I will have _____ .

2. By the end of this month, I will have _____ .

3. By the end of this year, I will have _____ .

4. By the end of the semester, the students will have _____ .

5. By the year 2000, I will have _____ .

6. By the year 2000, the people of the world will have _____ .

Used to + Simple Form of the Verb

Used to followed by the simple form of the verb expresses a past habit or custom that no longer occurs.

"He used to walk three miles to school every day." means that he walked three miles to school many times in the past, but he does not walk three miles to school now.*

"I used to smoke" means that I smoked in the past, but I do not smoke now.

Questions are formed by putting *did* before the subject and returning the verb to the simple form: *use.*

Did he use to live in that apartment?

Negative statements are rare.

EXERCISES

Here are some things that Frank and his wife Martha did in the past, and some things they do now. Construct a single sentence with *used to* + simple verb that expresses the meaning of the two sentences given.

EXAMPLE: Frank was fat. Now he is thin.

Frank used to be fat.

In the past	**Now**
1. Frank weighed 210 pounds.	He weighs 175 pounds.
2. Frank was single.	He is married.
3. Frank ate all his meals in a restaurant.	He always eats at home.
4. He lived in the city.	He lives in the suburbs.
5. He played baseball on weekends.	He doesn't play baseball.

* Do not confuse this with the expression "He is used to walking three miles to school every day," which will be discussed in Mini-grammar 5.

6. Martha worked in an office.   She sells real estate.

7. Martha typed letters all day.   She doesn't type letters.

8. She worked full-time.   She works part-time.

9. Martha lived with her parents.   She lives with her husband.

10. Frank and Martha went to the   They watch movies on television.
movies every Saturday.

11. Frank and Martha's baby son   He knows how to walk.
crawled on the floor.

12. Frank and Martha's daughter   She goes to elementary school.
went to nursery school.

Be Used to + verb + -ing

Adverbs of Frequency

I. Be used to + verb + -ing

When *used to* is preceded by *is, am,* or *are* and is followed by the simple form of the verb + *-ing,* it expresses a repeated action in the present. The person doing the action is accustomed to it and considers it normal.

"He is used to walking several miles to school now" means that he is accustomed to walking that distance. The situation is normal and not strange in any way.

"I am used to drinking two cups of coffee for breakfast" means that I am accustomed to drinking two cups of coffee. It is my habit.

Questions are formed by putting *is, am,* or *are* before the subject.

Is he used to walking to school?

Are the children used to playing indoors in wintertime?

Negatives are formed by adding *not (n't)* after *is, am,* or *are.*

He isn't used to walking to school when it is raining hard.

The children aren't used to playing in the house all day.

I'm not used to drinking tea for breakfast.

If the action indicated by the verb is understood or has been previously mentioned, the verb may be omitted and a noun phrase or a pronoun may follow *used to.*

All of us know that Max is always driving big cars.

Max is used to big cars. (driving big cars)

He is used to them. (driving them)

EXERCISES

In the following sentences change the phrase *accustomed to* to *used to.* Your sentence will mean the same as the sentence given. Sentences with *used to* are more common.

> **EXAMPLE:** Max is accustomed to driving fast.
>
> *Max is used to driving fast.*

1. Mr. M. isn't accustomed to making his own breakfast.

2. Mrs. M. is accustomed to getting up early to make breakfast for her husband.

3. Mr. M. is accustomed to buttered toast and two cups of coffee for breakfast.

4. He is not accustomed to putting bread in the toaster or making coffee.

5. Are some husbands accustomed to making their own breakfast?

6. Grandpa Smith is accustomed to telling his grandchildren how to behave.

7. His grandchildren are accustomed to more modern ideas.

8. Tommy is accustomed to asking a lot of questions.

9. Tommy's mother is accustomed to Tommy's questions.

10. Are most adults accustomed to answering small children's questions?

II. Adverbs of frequency

Adverbs of frequency are words that tell how often something happens. These are the most common:

Affirmative	Negative
always	never
almost always	hardly ever
usually	rarely
frequently	seldom
often	
sometimes	
occasionally	

The position of adverbs of frequency in a sentence is determined by the verb and by the meaning or emphasis intended.

A. In affirmative sentences in which the main verb is a form of *be* (*am, is, are, was, were*) the adverb of frequency follows the main verb.

The train is seldom full.

The teacher is sometimes late.

B. In affirmative sentences in which the main verb is not *be*, the adverb of frequency precedes the main verb. If there are auxiliary verbs, the adverb of frequency comes after the first auxiliary.*

He usually reads his newspaper on the train.

Tommy can often ask a hundred questions in one afternoon.

We have never gone swimming in the ocean.

C. When affirmative adverbs of frequency appear in negative statements, these guidelines apply:*

Always follows the negative (*not*, *n't*):

The children don't always study in the afternoon.

It isn't always warm in March.

Frequently, *sometimes*, and *occasionally* come before the negative:

Grandpa Smith's grandchildren frequently don't listen to his advice.

Tommy's mother sometimes isn't ready to answer all of Tommy's questions.

Often and *usually* come either before or after the negative:

He doesn't often go.   He often doesn't go.

She isn't usually late.   She usually isn't late.

---

* Except for *always*, affirmative adverbs of frequency may also be placed at the beginning of a sentence for emphasis: "Sometimes the teacher is late. Usually she is on time."
    Some affirmative adverbs of frequency may also be placed at the end of a sentence: "The teacher is late sometimes."
* Negative adverbs of frequency (*seldom*, *rarely*, *hardly ever*, and *never*) do not occur in statements that are already negative.

WRONG: Mr. M. doesn't never drive to work.
RIGHT: Mr. M. never drives to work.

EXERCISES

Insert the adverb of frequency in the following sentences. For some sentences more than one answer may be possible.

> **EXAMPLES:** (seldom)   Jeff tells jokes.
> *Jeff seldom tells jokes.*
> (usually)   The food is good.
> *The food is usually good.*
> (always)   He doesn't study after dinner.
> *He doesn't always study after dinner.*

(often)   **1.** Rick writes letters to his parents.

(hardly ever)   **2.** Roger is absent from class.

(always)   **3.** Tommy watches television Saturday mornings.

(rarely)   **4.** The Thompsons eat in expensive restaurants.

(frequently)   **5.** Susan doesn't eat breakfast.

(usually)   **6.** She eats a candy bar at 10:00 am.

(often)   **7.** She is hungry at noon.

(occasionally)   **8.** The teacher is late for class.

(seldom)   **9.** They have been to the museum.

(usually)   **10.** Steve doesn't wear a tie.

(rarely)   **11.** Tom has enough money.

(never)   **12.** Maria speaks English at home.

(always)   **13.** Maria speaks English at work.

(sometimes)   **14.** Maria speaks English with friends.

Special Meanings of <u>Make</u>, <u>Let</u>, and <u>Have</u>

In sentences in which another verb follows *make, let,* or *have,* the second verb is put in simple form.

>Mrs. Brown always makes the children do their homework. (*Do* is in simple form.)

>Mr. Brown had the mechanic fix his car. (*Fix* is in simple form.)

>The teacher will let the students be a few minutes late tomorrow. (*Be* is in simple form.)

The verbs *make* and *have* in these sentences show that one person is causing another person to do something. Usually the person causing the action has some authority over the other person—a boss, a teacher, a parent. *Make* suggests the use of either physical or psychological force. *Have* is often used when we employ or hire someone to do something for us.*

Let is used to express the idea of giving someone permission or allowing someone to do something.

EXERCISES

Change the following sentences, replacing the words *allow* or *permit* by *let; employ* or *hire* by *have;* and *force* by *make.* Remember to change the next verb in the sentences to the simple form (without *to*). Your new sentences will have approximately the same meaning as the sentences given.

>**EXAMPLE:** Tommy's mother *allowed* him *to play* outdoors.

>Tommy's mother *let* him *play* outdoors.

1. The Browns *hired* a plumber *to fix* their sink.

2. Tommy's mother *forced* Tommy *to pick up* his toys.

3. Tommy's mother doesn't *allow* Tommy *to cross* the street by himself.

---

* In informal style, *get* followed by *to* + the simple form of the verb can also be used to talk about someone causing someone else to do something. *Get* usually suggests persuasion rather than force: "Susan gets her friend to translate letters from her cousin in Brazil." "The children got their mother to bake them a cake."

4. The Blantons *employed* an architect *to design* their new house.

5. The policeman *forced* the thief *to drop* the gun.

6. The teacher doesn't *permit* the students *to write* in pencil.

7. She doesn't *force* them *to type* their homework.

8. The old man *employed* a lawyer *to draw up* his will.

9. The Browns didn't *hire* a painter *to paint* the kitchen; they did it themselves.

10. Her boss *allows* Mrs. Brown *to leave* work a little early three days a week.

Wishes, Hopes, and Advice about Present and Future Events

I. Wishes about present events

Usually people talk about real events in the world around them, but sometimes they like to talk about things that they know are impossible, almost impossible (improbable), or contrary to fact. A person may know the facts of a situation, but he may not like those facts. For example, a man may know that he has very little money, but he would like to have more, and he might say:

I wish I had a lot of money now.

Notice that the verb after *wish* is in past *tense* form, but the sentence is really talking about present *time*. (It will be easier for you if you think of *tense* and *time* as different things. *Time* is part of the real world. *Tense* is only in the grammar. Usually English and other languages use past tense to talk about past time—but not always.)

The combination of *wish* and the past *tense* form of another verb shows that the speaker is talking about something he knows is impossible or contrary to fact at the present time.

When the verb following *wish* in a sentence is some form of the verb *be*, we may sometimes choose between two possible past tense forms. For example, suppose that Mrs. Green is forty years old today. We might say:

A. She wishes (that) she *was* twenty. (informal style)
or
B. She wishes (that) she *were* twenty. (formal style)*

Sentence A is used by many educated English speakers in everyday speech. Sentence B is preferred for formal speech and writing.

Informal Style	**Formal Style**
(Use *was* after singular; use *were* after plural.)	(Use *were* after singular and plural.)
I wish (that) I was twenty.	I wish (that) I were twenty.
I wish (that) she was twenty.	I wish (that) she were twenty.

* *That* is optional.

| They wish (that) she was twenty. | They wish (that) she were twenty. |
| They wish (that) they were twenty. | They wish (that) they were twenty. |

EXERCISES

Assume that the sentences given below are statements of fact. Construct your own sentences expressing wishes in response to the facts. More than one answer is correct in each case. Be sure that the verb after *wish* is in past tense form.

> **EXAMPLE:** Mr. Peters is unhappy about his job. (fact)
>
> ### Possible wishes
> He wishes he had a better job.
>
> He wishes he could change jobs.
>
> He wishes he didn't have to work.
>
> He wishes he $\left\{ \begin{array}{c} \text{was} \\ \text{were} \end{array} \right\}$ happy about his job.

1. Mr. Peters doesn't like his boss.

2. His boss doesn't like him.

3. Mr. Peters doesn't get paid very well.

4. His work isn't interesting; he does the same thing all day.

5. He always eats lunch in the company cafeteria; the food isn't very good.

6. He has to wait in line a long time.

7. The coffee is always cold and not strong enough.

8. The cashier is always rude.

9. When he finishes work, he always has a headache.

10. His friends worry about him.

II. Wishes about future events

Of course no one knows exactly what will happen in the future, but we often use *wish* to talk about future events that we do not think will actually take place. When a clause after *wish* refers to the future, we usually use *would*, *could*, or *were going to.**

What the speaker thinks will happen	Speaker's wish
It will rain tomorrow.	I wish it wouldn't rain.
My friend probably can't come to the party next Saturday.	I wish he could come.
I don't think I am going to see you tomorrow.	I wish I were going to see you.

EXERCISES

The sentences given tell what the speaker thinks is really going to happen in the future. Construct your own sentences expressing wishes. More than one answer is correct in each case.

> EXAMPLE: **What the speaker thinks will happen**
> The price of food will be higher next year.
>
> **Wishes**
> I wish prices wouldn't get higher.
>
> I wish my salary would go up.
>
> I wish the government could stop inflation.

1. The tuition at Joe's college is going to be higher next year.

2. Joe is going to work longer hours at his part-time job.

---

* With some verbs it is also possible to use *were* followed by the present participle or the simple past tense after *wish* to talk about future events.

I wish you were coming with us tomorrow.
I wish they wanted to go with us next weekend.

Would is not used when the subject of the clause and the subject of *wish* are the same.

3. He can't see his friends very often next semester.

4. He is going to be tired a lot of the time.

5. He can't take some of the courses he wants.

6. It will take him longer to graduate.

III. Wishes and hopes

Joyce goes to visit her friend Bob in the hospital. Bob was in a bad car accident recently, and Joyce knows that he feels terrible. She is unhappy about his condition and says to him:

> I wish you felt better.   (Fact: Bob really feels terrible, and Joyce knows it.)

Joyce goes to visit Bob again. She hasn't seen him for two weeks, but she has heard that he is making great progress. This time she says to him:

> I hope you feel better.   (Joyce thinks it is possible that Bob feels better.)

We use *wish* and the past tense of another verb to talk about present or future events that we think are impossible, almost impossible (improbable), or contrary to fact.

We use *hope* and the present tense of another verb to talk about present or future events that we think are possible.

> EXAMPLES: **Present events**
>
> I wish it wasn't raining. (I know that in fact it is raining.)
>
> I hope it isn't raining. (It is possible that it is raining. I don't know.)
>
> **Future Events**
>
> I wish my sister could visit me next month. (I don't think she can visit me.)
>
> I hope my sister can visit me next month. (It is possible that she can.)

EXERCISES

Complete each of the following statements, using either *wish* or *hope*.

1. It's been raining all day; I _____ it stops soon.

2. Mr. Valentino won't study; I _____ he would.

3. Roberto is looking for his keys right now; I _____ he finds them.

4. Judy thinks her exam is going to be hard; I _____ she won't fail.

5. My parents are not in this country; I _____ they were.

6. I can't go back to visit them next year; I _____ I could.

7. They might come to visit me; I _____ they will.

IV. Giving advice about present and future events using should, ought to, and had better

When people want to give advice about present or future events they often use *should, ought to,* or *had better. Should* and *ought to* have the same meaning. "You should stop smoking" and "You ought to stop smoking" both mean "It would be a good idea for you to stop smoking." The speaker is not sure the advice will be followed.

Had better is stronger and may imply a warning or threat of possible bad consequences if the advice is not taken.*

EXERCISES

Give advice in the following situations by using *should* (*shouldn't*), *ought to,* or *had better* (*had better not*).†

EXAMPLE: I think I'm catching a cold.

You ought to take better care of yourself.

You shouldn't go outside again without a coat.

You'd better see a doctor; this is the third cold you've had this year.

---

* An even stronger expression of advice (necessity) would be: "You must stop smoking" or "You have to stop smoking." See Mini-grammar 11.

† The negative of *ought to* is *ought not to* (*oughtn't to*). It is less frequently used than *shouldn't.*

1. Jim wants to meet more people.

2. The library doesn't have the book that I need for class.

3. I have the hiccups.

4. The car is almost out of gas.

5. I'm bored.

6. Many of the students have difficulty with English spelling.

7. I'd like to find a better job.

8. Roger doesn't know how to cook.

Wishes about Past Events

Possibility in the Past

I. Wishes about past events

Sometimes people talk about things that they wish had happened in the past, but which they know did not happen. For example, the Thompsons did not buy a new car last year because they did not have enough money then. Now they feel sorry.

The Thompsons wish that they had bought a new car last year.

The wish is contrary to fact. The Thompsons know that they did not in fact buy a new car.

Susan was not invited to a party last week. She is unhappy about it now.

Susan wishes she had been invited to the party.

Notice that the verbs after *wish* are *had* and a past participle.* The use of *wish* followed by *had* and a past participle shows that the speaker is talking about something he knows did not in fact happen in the past. The wish is contrary to fact.

EXERCISES

The sentences that are given state facts about events that happened in the past. In each case, construct your own sentence expressing a wish that is contrary to that fact. Be sure that you use *had* and a past participle. More than one answer may be correct.

> **EXAMPLE:** Lois had a bad day yesterday.
>
> *She wishes she had had a good day.*
>
> *She wishes she had been happy yesterday.*
>
> *She wishes everything had not gone wrong yesterday.*

1. Lois woke up late yesterday morning. She wishes _____ .

* See pages 156–59 for irregular past participles.

2. She forgot to set her alarm clock the night before. She wishes

_____ .

3. She spilled coffee on her new dress. She wishes _____ .

4. She burned the toast when she made her breakfast. She wishes

_____ .

5. Her breakfast tasted terrible. She wishes _____ .

6. Her new car didn't start. She wishes _____ .

7. She had to take the bus to work. She wishes _____ .

8. Lois was an hour late to work. She wishes _____ .

9. Her boss yelled at her. She wishes _____ .

10. Her friend called to cancel their date. She wishes _____ .

11. She lost her purse. She wishes _____ .

12. She had a terrible headache when she got home. She wishes

_____ .

13. Yesterday was Friday the 13th. She wishes _____ .

II. Possibility in the past using <u>could</u> + <u>have</u> + past participle

Sometimes we want to talk about an event or an action that was possible in the past but did not in fact happen. For example, it was possible for the Thompsons to go on vacation last year. They had the time and the money, but they decided not to go.

They could have gone on vacation last year (but they didn't).*

It was possible for Susan to study math last night. Her math book was at home and she had time, but she decided to go to the movies instead.

Susan could have studied her math last night (but she didn't).*

* The words in parentheses are understood but are not usually said.

Notice that the verbs used to express unfulfilled possibility in the past are *could* followed by *have* and the past participle.

EXERCISES

The following sentences talk about events that happened in the past. Construct a sentence of your own telling about another event that was possible but that did not happen. Use *could* + *have* + the past participle.

> **EXAMPLE:** I didn't wear my coat yesterday. It was in the closet.
>
> *I could have worn my coat yesterday.*

1. George didn't invite Alice to the party last week. She was free.

2. Peter didn't pass the test. He had time to study, but he watched television instead.

3. Henry didn't eat breakfast yesterday. There was food in the refrigerator.

4. Mike didn't write to his parents yesterday. There were paper, pens, envelopes, and stamps in his desk drawer.

5. I didn't put any gas in the car this morning. I drove right by a gas station, and I had ten dollars in my wallet.

6. I didn't like the sandwich I ordered at the restaurant. There were lots of other things on the menu.

7. My pen ran out of ink. The student next to me had two pens.

8. Jeff wasn't feeling very well yesterday. His doctor was in his office.

Future Conditions Using <u>If</u>

I. Future conditions using <u>if</u> (real)

> If she goes to the party tomorrow, Susan will see her friend.

The sentence above has two clauses. Each clause has a subject and a verb. In the clause beginning with *if* the verb is in the present tense: *goes*. In the other clause the verbs are *will* and *see*. We can reverse the order of the clauses without changing the meaning.

> Susan *will see* her friend if she *goes* to the party tomorrow.

These sentences talk about a real condition. The speaker believes that it is possible that Susan will go to the party.*
Here are some other sentences of the same type.

> If they *take* a vacation next summer, they *will go* to Mexico.

> If the music *is* fast, he *will dance*.

> I *will tell* you the answer if I *know* it.

Notice that the verb in the clause beginning with *if* is always in the present tense, and that the verbs in the other clause are always *will* and the simple form.

EXERCISES

Fill in the blank with the correct form of the verb. Remember that the verb in the "if" clause is always in the present tense and that the verbs in the other clause are always *will* and the simple form.

(see, tell)   **1.** If I _____see_____ my friend tomorrow, I _____will_____
_____tell_____ him the news.

---

* If the speaker is certain that Susan will go to the party, he might say, "When she goes to the party, Susan will see her friend."

(have, lend)   **2.** If he _____ a pen, he _____
                  _____ it to you.

(be, buy)   **3.** If the shoes _____ on sale next week, I
                  _____ _____ them.

(write, know)   **4.** I _____ _____ if I _____ the
                  address.

(lend, have)   **5.** She _____ _____ you ten dollars if she
                  _____ enough money.

(be, receives)   **6.** She _____ _____ at the party, if she
                  _____ an invitation.

II. Future conditions using _if_ (contrary to fact)

> If she went to the party tomorrow, Susan would see her friend. (Susan will not go to the party.)*

Sometimes (as in the example above) we talk about events that we know are not going to happen, or things that we know are not real. Here are some more examples:

> If they _took_ a vacation next summer, they _would go_ to Mexico. (They are not going to take a vacation next summer.)*

> If the music _were_ fast, he _would dance_. (The music is not fast.) †

> I _would tell_ you the answer if I _knew_ it. (I don't know the answer.)

> If I _were_ you, I _wouldn't take_ that course. (I am not you.)

Notice the verbs used to talk about unreal, impossible, or contrary-to-fact conditions in present or future time. The verb in the clause beginning with _if_ is the same as that usually used for the past tense. The verbs in the other clause are always _would_ and the simple form.

---

* The words in parentheses are understood but are not said.
† In formal English _were_ is preferred in all persons for expressing unreal conditions. Informally many English speakers use _was_ after first and third person singular subjects.

EXERCISES

Fill in the blanks with the correct form of the verb needed to express an unreal or contrary-to-fact condition. The verb in the clause beginning with *if* should be in the past tense. The verbs in the other clause are *would* and the simple form.

(see, tell) **1.** If I _____saw_____ my friend tomorrow, I ____would____ _____tell_____ him the news. (I will not see my friend.)

(have, lend) **2.** If he _____ a pen, he _____ _____ it to you. (He doesn't have a pen.)

(be, buy) **3.** If the shoes _____ on sale next week, I _____ _____ them. (I don't think the shoes will be on sale.)

(write, know) **4.** I _____ _____ if I _____ the address. (I don't know the address.)

(lend, have) **5.** She _____ _____ you ten dollars if she _____ enough money. (She doesn't have enough money.)

(be, receives) **6.** She _____ _____ at the party, if she _____ an invitation. (I don't think she received an invitation)

(be, do) **7.** If I _____ you, I _____ _____ the homework a little more carefully. (I am not you.)

(drive, be) **8.** I _____n't _____ so fast if I _____ you. (I am not you.)

Revising the Past: <u>Would Have</u> and <u>Should Have</u>

I. Past conditions using <u>if</u> (contrary to fact)

It may seem strange, but people often talk about events that did not happen in the past. These are some examples:

If she *had gone* to the party last week, Susan *would have seen* her friend. (Susan did not go to the party last week.)*

If they *had taken* a vacation last summer, they *would have gone* to Mexico. (They didn't take a vacation last summer.)

If the music *had been* fast, he *would have danced.* (The music was not fast.)

I *would have told* you the answer if I *had known* it. (I didn't know the answer.)

Notice the verbs used to talk about unreal or contrary-to-fact conditions in past time. The verbs in the clause beginning with *if* are *had* and a past participle. The verbs in the other clause are *would* and *have* and a past participle.

EXERCISES

Fill in the blanks with the correct form of the verb needed to express an unreal or contrary-to-fact condition. You will be talking about events that did not take place in the past. The verbs in the *if* clause are *had* and a past participle. The verbs in the other clause are *would, have,* and a past participle.

(see, tell) **1.** If I ____had____ ____seen____ my friend yesterday, I ____would____ ____have____ ____told____ him the news. (I didn't see my friend yesterday.)

(have, lend) **2.** If he _____ _____ a pen that day, he _____ _____ _____ it to you. (He didn't have a pen.)

* The words in parentheses are understood but are not said.

125

(be, buy)　　**3.** If the shoes ＿＿＿＿＿＿＿ ＿＿＿＿＿＿＿ on sale last
　　　　　　　　week, I ＿＿＿＿＿＿ ＿＿＿＿＿＿ ＿＿＿＿＿＿
　　　　　　　　them. (The shoes weren't on sale.)

(write, know)　**4.** I ＿＿＿＿＿＿ ＿＿＿＿＿＿ ＿＿＿＿＿＿ if I
　　　　　　　　＿＿＿＿＿＿ ＿＿＿＿＿＿ the address. (I didn't
　　　　　　　　know the address.)

(lend, have)　　**5.** She ＿＿＿＿＿＿ ＿＿＿＿＿＿ ＿＿＿＿＿＿ you
　　　　　　　　ten dollars if she ＿＿＿＿＿＿ ＿＿＿＿＿＿ enough
　　　　　　　　money. (She didn't have enough money.)

II. Giving advice about past events using should + have + a past participle

Sometimes people like to give advice after it is too late to use it. For example, if you failed a test the teacher might say:

> You should have studied.

Or perhaps you slipped and fell on the ice and your friend tells you:

> You shouldn't have been in such a hurry.

Or you get sick because you went out without your overcoat, and the doctor tells you:

> You should have worn your overcoat.

Of course it is too late to follow any of this advice. The situation is like that of the man in the story who locked his barn door after his horse had been stolen.

Notice that the form used for giving advice about events that have already happened is *should* + *have* + the past participle of the verb.

EXERCISES

Give advice about the following situations. Use *should* + *have* + a past participle.

　　EXAMPLE: Alice forgot her umbrella. It was raining.

> *She should have remembered her umbrella.*

1. Tommy ate too much candy. He was sick yesterday evening.

2. You left the car keys in the ignition. Someone stole your car.

3. Peter told a lie. He felt sorry later.

4. Mrs. Thompson forgot to watch the soup she was cooking. The soup burned.

5. I forgot to put gas in the car. It wouldn't start.

6. Joe packed his suitcase. He left the toothpaste on the bathroom sink.

7. I didn't buy any food this morning. I need to cook dinner.

8. Jim didn't set his alarm clock last night. He overslept this morning.

9. Harry studied Lesson 15. The test he took this morning was on Lesson 16.

10. Jim was in a car accident. He was driving very fast.

Must and Have to to Express Necessity

Necessity or strong obligation can be expressed in present time affirmative statements and questions by either *must* or *have to* (or *has to*) followed by the simple form of the verb.

You must stop at the red light.*
or
You have to stop at the red light. †

Sally must cook dinner tonight.
or
Sally has to cook dinner tonight.

In affirmative statements and questions there is little or no difference in meaning between *must* and *have to* used to express necessity. *Have to* is used more often than *must*.

Used in negative statements *must* and *have to* have different meanings. "He doesn't have to take the medicine" means that it is not necessary for him to take the medicine. He may take it if he wants to, but there is no obligation for him to do so.

On the other hand, "He must not take the medicine" means that he is not allowed to take the medicine, or that he is forbidden to do so.

In past time only *had to* can be used to express necessity.

I had to stop at all the red lights when I drove into the city yesterday.

Sally had to cook dinner last night.

---

* *Must* does not always express necessity. Another common meaning of *must* is explained in Mini-grammar 12.
† Do not confuse *have to* with other uses of the the verb *have*.

    He has a car. (*Have* is the main verb.)
    They have gone home. (*Have* is an auxiliary.)
    Mr. Brown had the mechanic fix his car. (*Have* expresses the idea of causing something to be done. See Mini-grammar 6.)
    You had better see a doctor. (See Mini-grammar 7.)

129

EXERCISES

A. Construct sentences having approximately the same meaning as the sentences given. Use either *must* or *have to* in your sentences.

> **EXAMPLES:** It is necessary for Roger to get up early.
>
> *Roger must get up early.*
>
> *Roger has to get up early*
>
> Is it necessary for people to exercise every day?
>
> *Must people exercise every day?*
>
> *Do people have to exercise every day?*

1. It is necessary for all drivers to obey the traffic laws.

2. It is necessary for her to see the doctor.

3. Is it necessary for me to call Tom before visiting him?

4. Is it necessary for us to go shopping today?

5. Is it necessary for me to have a library card to use the library?

6. It is necessary to come to class on time.

7. Is it necessary for Mrs. Brown to send the letter by airmail?

8. It is necessary for Rick to pay his bills at the end of the month.

9. It is necessary for travelers to have a passport to go to another country.

10. It is necessary for students to relax sometimes.

B. Construct sentences having approximately the same meaning as the sentences given. Use *don't have to* or *doesn't have to* in your sentences.

> **EXAMPLE:** It is not necessary for Susan to get up early on weekends.
>
> *Susan doesn't have to get up early on weekends.*

1. It is not necessary for students to work all the time.

2. It is not necessary for Tom to wear glasses.

3. It is not necessary for travelers to have passports to travel in their own countries.

4. It is not necessary for students to come to class an hour early.

5. It is not necessary for students to know every word in the dictionary to speak English.

6. It is not necessary for Mrs. Brown to send a telegram.

7. It is not necessary for you to go to the hospital.

8. It is not necessary for Roger to call his girl friend every day.

C. Construct sentences having approximately the same meaning as the sentences given. Use *had to* to express necessity in past time.

> **EXAMPLE:** It was necessary for Rick to get a passport before he left his country.
>
> *Rick had to get a passport before he left his country.*

1. It was necessary for Anne to pay tuition before she entered the university.

2. It was necessary for the Browns to call the plumber to fix their sink yesterday.

3. It was necessary for Liz to take a test before she got her driver's license.

4. It was necessary for Tom to return some books to the library before he could take out new ones.

5. It was necessary for Mrs. Brown to pay for the groceries by check because she didn't have enough cash.

Must and Might to Express Inferences

I. Inferences about present or future events using must

Mini-grammar 11 discussed one meaning of *must. Must* can also be used to express an inference or a guess based on the facts of a situation.

> Fact: Henry and Bob work in the same office.

Inference: Henry must know Bob.

> Fact: A few minutes ago Audrey left work suddenly to go to the doctor. She looked pale.

Inference: She must be sick.

> Fact: No one answers the telephone at the Stephens' house.

Inference: They must not be home.

> Fact: The woman is wearing a ring on the third finger of her left hand.

Inference: She must be married.

When we make an inference using *must*, we believe that our guess is correct. The facts point to no other logical conclusion.

II. Inferences about present or future events using might

We use *might* + simple verb to express an inference or a guess based on the facts of a situation that we are much less cerain of. We believe that it is possible that our guess is correct, but we do not really know.

> Fact: Jim and Peter work in the same city.

Inference: Jim might know Peter.*

> Fact: Susan looks a little tired.

Inference: Susan might be sick.

* *May* is also used to express inferences that the speaker is not certain of: "Jim may know Peter."

133

EXERCISES

A. Make inferences about present or future events based on the facts that are given. You are almost certain that your inferences are correct. You may use the cues given in parentheses to construct your sentences.

> **EXAMPLE:** The car doesn't run. (be out of gas)
>
> *It must be out of gas.*

1. The Thompsons are getting a loan from the bank. (need money)

2. Henry is packing his suitcase. (be going on a trip)

3. Paul is looking at a Spanish newspaper. (read Spanish)

4. Anne and Sarah are always together. (be friends)

5. No one is wearing a coat. (be warm outside)

B. Again make inferences about present or future events or states based on the facts that are given. This time you are less certain that your inferences are correct.

> **EXAMPLE:** Jim isn't home.
>
> *He might be at the movies.*

1. Peter has been to Mexico. (know Spanish)

2. That dog is barking. (bite someone)

3. That store has a lot of sales. (have shirts on sale)

4. Susan isn't in school today. (be sick)

5. Roger is looking at travel magazines. (go on a trip next summer)

III. Inferences about past events

We express inferences about past events by using *must* + *have* + past participle if we are almost certain our inference is correct.

Fact: Henry and Bob worked in the same office ten years ago.

Inference: Henry must have known Bob.

Fact: No one answered the telephone at the Jackson's house last night.

Inference: They must not have been at home.

We express inference about past events that we are less certain of by using *might* + *have* + past participle.

Fact: Jim and Peter worked in the same city several years ago.

Inference: Jim might have known Peter.*

Fact: The Jacksons weren't home last night.

Inference: They might have gone to the movies.

EXERCISES

A. Make inferences about past events based on the facts that are given. You are almost certain that your inferences are correct. Use the cues given in parentheses to construct your sentences.

EXAMPLE: The sidewalk was wet this morning. (rain /last night)

It must have rained last night.

1. My keys are not in my purse. (leave/them at home)

2. Susan ate a big dinner last night. (be/hungry)

3. People didn't laugh at Steve's joke. (not think/it was funny)

4. Sarah was late for school yesterday. (miss/the bus)

5. Jim got all the answers right on the test. (study)

---

* It is also possible to say "Jim may have known Peter."

B. Again make inferences about past events based on the facts that are given. This time you are less certain that your inferences are correct.

> **EXAMPLE:** Susan looked a little tired last week.
>
> *She might have been sick.*

1. Mrs. Thompson was late to work this morning. (miss/the bus)

2. The Thompsons didn't buy a new car last month. (not have/enough money)

3. Sally didn't sleep well last night. (be/worried)

4. Everyone was smiling when they left the party. (have/a good time)

5. Anne didn't answer my question. (not hear/me)

Past and Present Participles Used as Adjectives

Both past participles and present participles (verb + *ing*) can be used as adjectives. They modify nouns in the same way as other adjectives.

>Thunder often *frightens* children.
>>(verb)

>The *frightening* thunder disturbed the child.
>>(present participle *frightening* used as an adjective)

>The children are *frightened*.
>The *frightened* children ran to their mothers.
>>(past participle *frightened* used as an adjective)

Notice the usual difference in meaning between the present participle and the past participle when they are used as adjectives: the present participle expresses an active quality or a quality that affects people; the past participle expresses the corresponding passive quality.

Here are some other examples:

>Anne *charms* everyone.
>>(verb)

>Anne is a *charming* girl.

>Everyone is *charmed*.

>The professor *bored* the students.
>>(verb)

>The professor is *boring*.

>The *boring* professor kept on talking.

>The students are *bored*.

>The *bored* students went to sleep.

EXERCISES

Complete the following sentences with either the past participle or the present participle (verb + -*ing*) used as an adjective.

EXAMPLE: The experiment *interests* the scientists.

It is an *interesting* experiment.

The scientists are very *interested*.

1. Studying in the library all day *exhausted* Roberto.
Roberto was _____ from studying so hard.
The life of a student like Roberto is _____ .

2. The airplane crash *horrified* everyone at the airport.
The _____ spectators watched the plane fall to the ground.
The crash was _____ .

3. Steve *entertains* his guests by telling jokes.
Steve's jokes are _____ .
Most of the guests are _____ .

4. Circuses *excite* children.
The _____ children left the circus.
The trapeze act was the most _____ part of the circus.

5. The noise of the city *disturbs* Liz.
The _____ noises keep Liz from sleeping.
Liz is _____ when the noises of the city keep her awake.

6. Lana's behavior *irritates* all the other actors.
Lana's _____ behavior is well known.
The _____ actors refused to work with Lana.

7. The announcement of Sally's and Mike's marriage *surprised* Rick.
The announcement was _____ .
Rick was extremely _____ .

8. Last minute changes in class schedule always *confuse* students.
The last minute changes were very _____ .
The _____ students went to the wrong class.

Some Ways of Expressing Cause and Concession

I. Expressing cause: <u>because</u> and <u>because of</u>

The expressions *because* and *because of* introduce a cause of an event or situation. The result stated in the sentence is the expected or usual result.

> We stayed at home because the weather was terrible.
> (expected result)   (cause)

> We stayed at home because of the terrible weather.
> (expected result)   (cause)

The two sentences have similar meanings.
    Notice that *because* is followed by a clause containing both a subject and a verb; the clause is equivalent to a complete sentence: *The weather was terrible.* The expression *because of* is followed by a noun phrase only: *the terrible weather.*
    It is possible to reverse the order of these sentences without changing the meaning.

> Because the weather was terrible, we stayed home.

> Because of the terrible weather, we stayed home.

In this order a comma usually separates the two parts of the sentence.*
    Here are some more pairs of sentences. Notice the difference in the constructions following *because* and *because of.*

> Ted didn't buy the large car because it cost too much.
> Ted didn't buy the large car because of its cost.

> Sarah didn't buy the dress because it was too large.
> Sarah didn't buy the dress because of its size.†

---

* *Since* and *as* can be used in a way similar to *because:* "*Since* the weather was terrible, we stayed home." "*As* the weather was terrible, we stayed home."
    Due to can be used in a way similar to *because of:* "*Due to* the terrible weather, we stayed home."
† Sometimes the same idea must be expressed by different words in the noun phrase.

EXERCISES

In the following sentences change *because* to *because of*. Make all other necessary changes. Your sentences should have approximately the same meaning as the sentences given.

> **EXAMPLE:** Mrs. Thompson was late for work because the bus was slow.
>
> *Mrs. Thompson was late for work because of the slow bus.*

1. The stores were closed because it was a holiday.

2. Because he has an evening class, Jeff will be late to the party.

3. Because the drivers are on strike, there are few buses running in the city.

4. Anne didn't go back to the restaurant because the food was bad.

5. Because there was a snow storm, the plane was late.

6. No one felt like working that summer because it was hot.

7. Because the rooms were small, Rick didn't rent the apartment.

8. Because the room was noisy, the students couldn't hear the teacher.

9. Ted couldn't see the blackboard because his eyesight was poor.

10. Grandpa Smith fell because the sidewalks were icy.

II. Two ways of expressing concession: <u>although</u> and <u>in spite of</u>

When the expressions *although* and *in spite of* are used in one part of a sentence, the events talked about in the other part of the sentence are unexpected or unusual.

> We went for a walk, although the weather was terrible.
>
> We went for a walk, in spite of the terrible weather.
>
> (People don't usually go for walks when the weather is terrible.)

The two sentences have similar meanings.

Notice that *although* is followed by a clause containing both a subject and a verb; the clause is equivalent to a complete sentence: *The weather was terrible.* The expression *in spite of* is followed by a noun phrase only: *the terrible weather.**

Here are some more pairs of sentences with similar meanings. Notice the differences in the constructions that follow *although* and *in spite of.*

Ted didn't buy the car, although the price was low.

Ted didn't buy the car, in spite of the low price.

Although it is big, the suitcase isn't heavy.

In spite of its size, the suitcase isn't heavy.

EXERCISES

In the following sentences change *although* to *in spite of.* Make all other necessary changes. Your sentences should have approximately the same meaning as the sentences given.

EXAMPLE: Roger finished the assignment, although it was difficult.

Roger finished the assignment, in spite of its difficulty.

1. Anne bought a new sweater, although it was expensive.

2. Although he worked hard, Ben didn't get the raise he expected.

3. Although the weather was warm, Tommy's mother didn't take him to the beach.

4. Peter didn't get the job, although he was qualified.

5. Judy couldn't understand the professor, although he spoke slowly.

6. Although it was raining, Mrs. Thompson didn't take an umbrella.

---

* *Even though* and *though* can be used in a way similar to *although:* "We went for a walk, even though the weather was terrible." "We went for a walk, though the weather was terrible." *Despite* can be used in a way similar to *in spite of:* "We went for a walk, despite the terrible weather." It is possible to reverse the order of these sentences without changing the meaning.

7. Tommy climbed the tree, although it was dangerous.

8. Although it had good reviews, the movie was not popular.

9. Max drove fast, although the roads were slippery.

10. Sally didn't marry Rick, although she had promised to.

Comparisons of Equality and Inequality

I. Comparing two persons, things, or groups that are alike in some way

A. One way of comparing two persons, things, or groups that are alike is to use the pattern

$$as + \left\{ \begin{array}{l} \text{adjective} \\ \text{adverb} \end{array} \right\} + as$$

Roger's hair is as *long* as his brother's.
(adj.)

Maria is as *beautiful* as a movie star.
(adj.)

Mrs. Thompson drives as *carefully* as her husband does.
(adv.)

EXERCISES

Using the information given, construct a single sentence of comparison using the pattern:

$$as + \left\{ \begin{array}{l} \text{adjective} \\ \text{adverb} \end{array} \right\} + as$$

EXAMPLE: Peter is lazy. George is equally lazy.

George is as lazy as Peter.

1. The Thompsons' car is 8′6″ long. The Blantons' car is 8′6″ long.*

2. Jeff is 6′2″ tall. Jeff's brother is 6′2″ tall.

3. Sarah is intelligent. Anne is equally intelligent.

4. One musician is talented. Another musician is equally talented.

---

* 8′6″ = 8 feet, 6 inches.

143

5. My chemistry teacher speaks rapidly. My math teacher speaks just as rapidly.

6. Mr. Thompson's secretary types well. Mrs. Reynolds' secretary types equally well.

B. Another way of comparing persons, things, or groups that are alike in some way is to use this pattern:

the same + noun + *as*

Susan's book is the same *color* as Sarah's.
(noun)

Tommy is the same *age* as his best friend.
(noun)

This class meets at the same *time* as my other class.
(noun)

EXERCISES

Using the information given, construct a single sentence of comparison using the pattern

the same + noun + *as*

EXAMPLE: Ted's hair is red. Rick's hair is red. (color)

Ted's hair is the same color as Rick's.

1. The Thompsons' house has five rooms. The Blantons' house has five rooms. (size)

2. The girl from Argentina speaks Spanish. The girl from Columbia speaks Spanish too. (language)

3. Tommy is 3'6" tall. His best friend is 3'6" tall. (height)

4. Mr. Thompson makes $200 a week. Mr. Reynolds makes $200 a week. (salary)

5. The front window is 32" wide. The back window is also 32" wide. (width)

6. The lake is 10' deep. The river is 10' deep. (depth)

7. The wooden table is 4′ long. The metal table is 4′ long. (length)

8. My biology text is 128 pages long. My history text is 128 pages long. (length)

C. Still another way of comparing two persons, things, or groups that are alike in some way is to use the pattern

$$as \begin{Bmatrix} much \\ many \end{Bmatrix} + \text{noun} + as^*$$

Rick has as much *education* as Jeff has.
               (noun)

The Thompsons have as many *children* as the Reynolds do.
                           (noun)

EXERCISES

Using the information given, construct a single sentence of comparison using the pattern

$$as \begin{Bmatrix} much \\ many \end{Bmatrix} + \text{noun} + as$$

    EXAMPLE: The science building has three floors. The library has three floors.

    The science building has as many floors as the library.

1. The Siegal's have $10,000 in the bank. The Thompsons have $10,000 in the bank. (money)

2. Sarah has $10 in her wallet. Anne has $10 in her wallet. (dollars)

3. Roger has two roommates. Rick has two roommates.

4. Mr. M. drinks two cups of coffee for breakfast. Mrs. M. drinks two cups of coffee for breakfast.

5. Rick wrote a letter to his girlfriend every day. Roger wrote a letter to his girlfriend every day.

---

* *Many* is used before nouns that can be counted: dollars, rooms, hours. *Much* is used before nouns that are not countable: money, space, time.

II. Comparing two persons, things, or groups that are different in some way

There are many ways of comparing persons, things, or groups that are different from each other; adjectives or adverbs are often used in the comparison.

A. Most adjectives and adverbs of one syllable (*young, tall, fast*) or two syllables ending in *y* (*busy, happy, friendly*) form comparatives by adding *er* to the adjective or adverb followed by the word *than*.

Mrs. Reynolds is younger than her brother.

Roger is happier than he was last semester.

A few common adjectives and adverbs have irregular comparative forms.

Adjective	Comparative form	Adverb	Comparative form
good	better	well	better
bad	worse	badly	worse
far	farther		

The new secretary types better than the old one.

The weather was worse this weekend than last weekend.

EXERCISES

Using the information given, construct a single sentence expressing a comparison of inequality using the pattern

$$\left\{ \begin{matrix} \text{adjective} \\ \text{adverb} \end{matrix} \right\} + \text{-}er + than$$

EXAMPLE: Tommy is 3′6″ tall. Tommy's older brother is 4′ tall.

Tommy's brother is taller than Tommy.

1. Mrs. Thompson is 28 years old. Mrs. M. is 32 years old.

2. The Mississippi River is 2,350 miles long. The Missouri River is 2,464 miles long.

3. The restaurant is noisy. The cafeteria is very noisy.

4. Sarah is a good student. Ellie is a very good student.

5. Peter swims well. His sister swims very well.

6. Paul is a bad dancer. George is a very bad dancer.

7. One of my roommates plays the piano badly. Another roommate plays the piano very badly.

B. Comparisons using adjectives or adverbs of two syllables not ending in *y* or of three or more syllables use the pattern

$$more + \begin{Bmatrix} adjective \\ adverb \end{Bmatrix} + than$$

Lana is more beautiful than the other actresses in the film.

The new bookkeeper at Mr. M.'s bank is more accurate than the old one.

Mr. M. drives more carefully than Max does.

EXERCISES

Using the information given, construct a single sentence expressing a comparison of inequality using the pattern:

$$more + \begin{Bmatrix} adjective \\ adverb \end{Bmatrix} + than$$

EXAMPLE: Dogs are curious. Cats are usually very curious.

*Cats are usually more curious than dogs.**

1. Many children are inquisitive. Tommy is very inquisitive.

2. Most children's mothers are patient. Tommy's mother is very patient.

3. Mr. Thompson is an efficient worker. Mr. M. is a very efficient worker.

4. Mario speaks English fluently. Mr. Lee speaks English very fluently.

5. Rick is studious. Roger is very studious.

* Another way of expressing the same idea: *Dogs are usually less curious than cats.*

6. My physics teacher speaks clearly. My English teacher speaks very clearly.

7. Max's jokes are amusing. Steve's jokes are very amusing.

8. Serious movies are popular. Comedies are very popular.

C. Still another way of comparing two persons, things, or groups that are different in some way is to use the pattern

more + noun + *than*

The Davises have more children than the Thompsons.

The university library has more books than the college library.

EXERCISES

Using the information given, construct a single sentence expressing a comparison of inequality using the pattern

more + noun + *than*

EXAMPLE: Professor Jackson teaches three classes every day.

Professor Phillips teaches four classes every day.

Professor Phillips teaches more classes than Professor Jackson.

1. A 707 uses a lot of fuel. A 747 uses even more fuel.

2. My desk dictionary has 750 pages. The unabridged dictionary has 3,500 pages.

3. Tommy's sister asked ten questions yesterday. Tommy asked twenty-five questions.

4. Susan bought three fashion magazines this week. She bought two magazines last week.

5. The small grocery store sells four different brands of coffee. The supermarket sells ten different brands of coffee.

Superlatives

The superlative form is used to compare three or more persons, things, or groups that differ from one another.

A. One syllable adjectives and adverbs (young, tall, fast) and two syllable adjectives ending in y (busy, happy, friendly) form superlatives by adding *est* to the simple form of the adjective. The word *the* is placed before the superlative.

Simple form	Comparative	Superlative
young	younger	the youngest
busy	busier*	the busiest
fast	faster	the fastest
hard	harder	the hardest

A few common adjectives and adverbs have irregular comparative and superlative forms:

Simple form	Comparative	Superlative
good (adj.)	better	the best
well (adv.)	better	the best
bad (adj.)	worse	the worst
badly (adv.)	worse	the worst
far (adj. and adv.)	farther	the farthest

Tommy is the youngest of the three children in his family.

Max drives the fastest of all.

She is the worst typist I have ever seen.

---

* Y is changed to *i* when the *-er* or *-est* ending is added: *busy, busier, busiest; happy, happier, happiest.*

EXERCISES

Using the information given, construct a single sentence comparing three or more persons, things, or groups using the pattern:

$$the \begin{Bmatrix} \text{adjective} \\ \text{adverb} \end{Bmatrix} + \text{-est}$$

EXAMPLE: Liz is older than Anne or Ellie.

Liz is the oldest of the three.

Mr. M.'s secretary is busier than any other person in the office.

Mr. M.'s secretary is the busiest person in the office.

1. Mt. Everest is higher than any other mountain in the world.

2. Alice is thinner than Sarah or Susan.

3. Peter is taller than any other player on his basketball team.

4. Joe runs faster than Mike or Tom.

5. Joan sings better than the other girls in the chorus.

6. Max drives faster than any other Texan.

7. Ben plays the guitar better than Sally or Tom.

B. When adjectives (not ending in *-y*) or adverbs of two or more syllables are used to compare three or more persons, things, or groups that differ from one another, the words *the most* are put before the simple forms.

Simple form	Comparative	Superlative
careful	more careful	the most careful
carefully	more carefully	the most carefully
efficient	more efficient	the most efficient
efficiently	more efficiently	the most efficiently

Mr. M. is the most careful driver I know.

Mr. M. drives the most carefully of all the people I know.

Ms. Johnson is the most efficient worker in the office.

Ms. Johnson works the most efficiently of all the people in the office.

Least is the opposite of *most*.

Max is the least careful driver I know.

Betty is the least efficient worker in the office.

EXERCISES

Using the information given, construct a sentence comparing three or more persons, things, or groups using the pattern:

$$the\ most\ + \left\{ \begin{array}{l} adjective \\ adverb \end{array} \right\}$$

EXAMPLES: Roger is more serious than any other student in his class.

Roger is the most serious student in his class.

Juan speaks English more fluently than Tony or Lee.

Juan speaks English the most fluently of the three.

1. George was more famous than any other movie star of his time.

2. Jerry is more ambitious than George or Peggy.

3. Steve is more sociable than any of his friends.

4. Lana is more beautiful than any other actress in Hollywood.

5. Boris is more polite than any other actor.

6. Peggy dances more gracefully than Pat or Susan.

7. Joan answers the teachers questions more promptly than any of the other students.

C. When nouns are used to compare three or more persons, things, or groups, the pattern used is

the most + noun

the most students

the most education

The eleven o'clock class has the most students of any English class in the school.

Mrs. Davis has the most education of any of the teachers.

EXERCISES

Using the information given, construct a sentence using the pattern

the most + noun

EXAMPLE: Tommy asks more questions than either of his two brothers.

Tommy asks the most questions of the three.

1. The university library has more books than the high school library or the city library.

2. George's house has more rooms than any other house on the block.

3. The Frasers have more children than the Thompsons or the Browns.

4. Mr. Thompson takes more time for lunch than any other employee in the office.

5. Mr. Brown drinks more coffee than Mr. Thompson or Ms. Harris.

6. Mr. M. spends more money for lunch than Mr. Brown or Mr. Thompson.

Shortened Forms

Shortened forms (contractions) are normal in speech and in informal writing, such as letters to friends. Full forms are preferred for formal writing, such as school assignments or business letters.

In many negative sentences more than one shortened form is possible. Either form is correct, although one may be preferred by a particular group of English speakers. (Forms that are common in British usage but not in American usage are printed in italics.)

Full Form	**Shortened Forms**	

Be (present tense)

I am not	I'm not	_____ *
You (sing.) are not	You're not	You aren't
He is not	He's not	He isn't
She is not	She's not	She isn't
It is not	It's not	It isn't
We are not	We're not	We aren't
You (pl.) are not	You're not	You aren't
They are not	They're not	They aren't

Have (present tense) **as an auxiliary verb**

I have not	*I've not*	I haven't
You (sing.) have not	*You've not*	You haven't
He has not	*He's not*†	He hasn't
She has not	*She's not*†	She hasn't
It has not	*It's not*†	It hasn't
We have not	*We've not*	We haven't
You (pl.) have not	*You've not*	You haven't
They have not	*They've not*	They haven't

* *Aren't I?* is used for *Am I not?* in negative questions. *Ain't* is nonstandard.
† Notice that the shortened form of *is* is the same as the shortened form of *has*.

Have (past tense) **as an auxiliary verb**

I had not	*I'd not**	I hadn't
He had not	*He'd not*	He hadn't

(Forms with *you, she, it, we,* and *they* are constructed on the same pattern.)

Modal Auxiliaries   Only the forms with *I* are given. Forms with *you, he, she, it, we, they* are constructed on the same pattern.

I will not	*I'll not*	I won't
I would not	*I'd not**	I wouldn't
I cannot†	_____	I can't
I could not	_____	I couldn't
I may not	_____	*I mayn't‡*
I might not	_____	I mightn't
I shall not	_____	*I shan't*
I should not	_____	I shouldn't
I must not	_____	I mustn't
I ought not to	_____	I oughtn't to

Do

do not	don't
does not	doesn't
did not	didn't

* Notice that the shortened form of *had* is the same as the shortened form of *would*.
† Usually spelled as one word.
‡ Rare.

Regular and Irregular Verbs

Regular verbs

Most verbs are regular. Regular verbs have five forms: simple, past, past participle, third person singular present, and present participle (-*ing* form). Here are some examples of regular verbs.

Simple form	Past	Past part.	Third pers. sing. pres.	Present part.
talk	talked	talked	talks	talking
hope	hoped*	hoped*	hopes	hoping*
watch	watched	watched	watches†	watching
stop	stopped‡	stopped‡	stops	stopping‡
play	played	played	plays	playing
study	studied**	studied**	studies**	studying

You do not need to memorize regular verbs because you can construct all the forms if you know some simple rules and spelling exceptions.

RULES

1. To form the past and past participle, add -*ed* to the simple form. The past and past participle forms of regular verbs are always the same.

2. To form the third person singular present, add -*s* to the simple form.

3. To form the present participle, add -*ing* to the simple form.

SPELLING EXCEPTIONS

*If the simple form ends in *e*, drop the final *e* before adding -*ed* or -*ing* (*hope, hoped, hoping*).

†If the simple form ends in the letters *s*, *z*, *ch*, *sh*, or *x*, add -*es* to form the third person singular present (*watch, watches*). The letters *es* are also added to the irregular verbs *do* and *go* (*does, goes*).

155

‡ If the simple form ends in a single consonant preceded by a single vowel, the final consonant is doubled before adding -ed or -ing (stop, stopped, stopping). This rule applies to words whose simple form has only one syllable, and to multi-syllabic words ending in an accented syllable.

** If the simple form ends in y preceded by a consonant, change the y to an i before adding -ed (study, studied); and before adding -es to form the third person singular present (study, studies).

Irregular verbs

All irregular verbs with one exception (the verb be) also have only five forms. Here are some examples of irregular verbs.

Simple form	Past	Past part.	Third pers. sing. pres.	Present part.
go	went	gone	goes	going
bring	brought	brought	brings	bringing
swim	swam	swum	swims	swimming
lose	lost	lost	loses	losing
put	put	put	puts	putting
run	ran	run	runs	running

Notice that you do not have to memorize the third person singular present and present participle forms of irregular verbs. You can construct them from the same rules you used for regular verbs.* However, there is no way of telling what the past and past participle forms of irregular verbs are. They must be memorized.

Experts say that there are about 250 irregular verbs in English, but many of them are not used very often. It is much better to know the common irregular verbs perfectly than to try to memorize all of them.

---

* An exception is the third person singular present form of have: has.

The following are the most common irregular verbs. You probably already know many of them. You should learn the others well enough to be able to write and say them without error. Cover all but the simple form with a sheet of paper and check to see if you can write the irregular past and past participle forms for each verb. Check with your teacher to see that you can pronounce each form correctly.

Simple	Past	Past Part.	Simple	Past	Past Part.
become	became	become	eat	ate	eaten
beat	beat	beaten	fall	fell	fallen
bend	bent	bent	feed	fed	fed
bet	bet	bet	feel	felt	felt
bite	bit	bitten (bit)	fight	fought	fought
bleed	bled	bled	find	found	found
blow	blew	blown	fit	fit	fit
break	broke	broken	fly	flew	flown
bring	brought	brought	forget	forgot	forgotten
build	built	built	forgive	forgave	forgiven
burst	burst	burst	freeze	froze	frozen
buy	bought	bought	get	got	got (gotten)
catch	caught	caught	give	gave	given
choose	chose	chosen	go	went	gone
come	came	come	grow	grew	grown
cost	cost	cost	have	had	had
cut	cut	cut	hear	heard	heard
dig	dug	dug	hit	hit	hit
do	did	done	hold	held	held
draw	drew	drawn	hurt	hurt	hurt
drink	drank	drunk	keep	kept	kept
drive	drove	driven	know	knew	known

Simple	Past	Past Part.	Simple	Past	Past Part.
lay	laid	laid	shine	shone	shone
lead	led	led	shoot	shot	shot
lend	lent	lent	show	showed	shown
let	let	let			(showed)
lie (recline)*	lay	lain	shut	shut	shut
light	lit (lighted)	lit (lighted)	sing	sang	sung
make	made	made	sink	sank	sunk
mean	meant	meant	sit	sat	sat
meet	met	met	sleep	slept	slept
pay	paid	paid	slide	slid	slid
put	put	put	speak	spoke	spoken
quit	quit	quit	spend	spent	spent
read**	read	read	spring	sprang	sprung
ride	rode	ridden	stand	stood	stood
ring	rang	rung	steal	stole	stolen
rise	rose	risen	stick	stuck	stuck
run	ran	run	strike	struck	struck
say	said	said	swear	swore	sworn
see	saw	seen	sweep	swept	swept
seek	sought	sought	swim	swam	swum
sell	sold	sold	swing	swung	swung
send	sent	sent	take	took	taken
set	set	set	teach	taught	taught
shake	shook	shaken	tear	tore	torn

* *Lie* (to deliberately say something untrue) is regular: *lie, lied, lied.*
** Although all three forms are spelled alike, the pronunciation of the simple form differs from that of the past and past participle.

Simple	Past	Past Part.	Simple	Past	Past Part.
tell	told	told	weep	wept	wept
think	thought	thought	win	won	won
throw	threw	thrown	wind	winded	winded
understand	understood	understood		(wound)	(wound)
wake up	woke up	woken up	write	wrote	written
	(waked up)	(waked up)			
weave	wove	woven			
		(weaved)			

Do you know all these verbs? Write any verbs you missed on the chart below. Memorize the correct forms. Be strict with yourself. You should be aiming for 100% accuracy in knowing the most common irregular verbs.

PERSONAL REVIEW CHART

Simple form	Past	Past Participle

A special irregular verb: <u>be</u>

One irregular verb is different from all the others. The verb *be* has eight different forms. (Every other verb has no more than five different forms.)

Simple form: **be**

Present tense forms: **am, is, are***

I am	we are
you (sing.) are	you (pl.) are
he is	they are
she is	
it is	

Past tense forms: **was, were**†

I was	we were
you (sing.) were	you (pl.) were
he was	they were
she was	
it was	

Past participle: **been**

Present participle: **being**

---

* Every other regular and irregular verb has only two different present tense forms: The simple form is used after *I, you, we* and *they.* The third person singular present form is used after *he, she* and *it.*

† Every other regular and irregular verb has only one past form used after all persons.

INDEX OF STRUCTURE SKILLS

A 1
B 2
C 3
D 4
E 5
F 6
G 7
H 8
I 9
J 0